VIGNETTES OF HOPE
FROM A WOUNDED HEALER

MARY V. NELSON

Vignettes of Hope From a Wounded Healer
by Mary Nelson

ISBN 1-58169-224-2
For Worldwide Distribution
Printed in the U.S.A.

Axiom Press
P.O. Box 191540 • Mobile, AL 36619
800-367-8203

Note: The stories in this book are true.
Some names and details have been changed
in order to protect the privacy of those involved.

TABLE OF CONTENTS

DEDICATION

To May Gould Hiebert,

the angel God

sent to lead me to the truth

ACKNOWLEDGMENTS

With thanks to my communicative
God for this assignment. Thanks also to Lila
Shelburne, my editor,
and to Delores Bauer and Russell Irwin
for their invaluable input.

FOREWORD

After many years of groping for truth, I now praise the Lord for letting me experience the reality of II Corinthians 1:3-4, "Praise be to the God and Father of our Lord Jesus Christ, the Father of compassion and God of all comfort, who comforts us in all our troubles, so that we can comfort those in any trouble with the comfort we ourselves have received from God."

How I thank the Lord for the comfort I received from Him through the ministry He has opened to Mary. She has truly given to me, and many others, the same comfort she acquired from Christ when she received Him into her life after years of lonely and troubled searching. Through insights gained in her walk with the Lord, she led me to Him for cleansing and healing each wound I carried by carving out the lies and filling my gaping sores with healing truth.

Many of the stories in this book are mine and may be yours as well. The healing process is simple if you are willing to momentarily embrace the pain of a memory in order to be transformed for a lifetime. When going through the pain, you are not alone. There is One who goes with you, giving you courage and companionship. God will never abandon you. When you ask Him, He will reveal lies that have held you captive for years, then quickly flood your whole being with truth, emotionally disconnecting you from the crippling pain of untruths.

Some wonder what "hearing from the Lord" really means. God wants to communicate truth to us, and He will do this in a variety of ways. Sometimes He will show Himself as a minister to our needs, sometimes as a protector, and other times as a revealer of lies. In each case, God wants to breathe life into peoples' wounded hearts. Hope comes in knowing Jesus intimately. He is our breath of life, the reason this book has been written.

Life is a journey. Every day we all face challenges such as fear, insecurity, anger, and depression. We cannot be held in bondage to old lies and truly live in the present. A short trip to the past to dispel the lies which bind us, strengthens our spirits and souls for the tasks at hand.

There was a woman in Jesus' time who almost bled to death because of hemorrhaging (Lk. 8:43-48). She had been bleeding for twelve years, but no one could heal her. There were rules in those days that the Jews and non-believers followed. This woman, however, was desperate enough to challenge them. She came up behind Jesus and touched the edge of His cloak and immediately her bleeding stopped.

"Who touched me?" Jesus asked.

When everyone present denied the touch, Peter said, "Master, the people are crowding and pressing against You."

But Jesus said, "Someone touched Me. I know that power has gone from Me."

Then the woman, seeing that she could not go unnoticed, came trembling and fell at His feet. In the presence of all the people, she explained why she had touched Him and how she had been instantly healed. Then he said to her, "Daughter, your faith has healed you. Go in peace."

This book was birthed because Jesus calls women "daughter." He heals them emotionally because He accepts them. Family members and friends could not lie on the ailing woman's bed or sit where she sat. In those days there was little tolerance for a woman with this kind of ailment. Jesus, however, accepted her, giving her worth and emotional healing, and publicly called her a loving title that showed she was included in His family. This is happening today and is what so many women need. Jesus heals our emotions now just as He did in Bible times.

In these short "snapshots" of lives renewed by the transforming touch of God, Mary has drawn a vivid picture of restoration badly needed by the church today. She knows that God speaks to us in ways that each of us can perceive and hear, and that He brings healing and deliverance from our past. We seem to have lost the ability to find our emotional health in Jesus and instead seek relief in secular therapy, drugs, alcohol, and sex. Mary has reminded us that it is only God who can truly heal, and she does this by sharing with us her own personal experiences.

May this book of vignettes inspire you to surrender your wounded places to Him. May you move forward in the knowledge that God is alive, that He speaks to you personally and wants you free from the lies that hinder your walk with Him.

—*Delores Bauer*, artist and author of *Stories From the Irish Wilderness*

PREFACE

Many people don't know how God speaks to us and wonder, "Is He really talking to me or is this just an inspirational thought?" We just don't know! One example of how God speaks is as follows.

As Moses was tending his father-in-law's sheep in the desert, God spoke to him from a burning bush (Exodus 3:1-2). When Moses turned to see why the bush had not completely burned up, God said, "Moses, Moses!" From these words spoken by God directly to him, Moses got his marching orders to be the one who would lead the children of Israel out of Egypt.

Sometimes God will give us a new thought or an inspiring idea. Sometimes He speaks in an audible voice. Other times, like a bright light that is switched on, His glory becomes clear. It is only when we are truly quiet that we can hear His still, small voice through the bustle of everyday busyness.

As I have ministered to many people who had need of the Master's touch, it has been humbling to watch them receive His guidance and healing. After a lifetime of pain and hurt, God's Spirit rushed in to fill the hole in their hearts as they listened and received His words.

Chapter 1

Jesus Is Present, Not Far Away

Believing Lies

Gazing out the window of the train rocking raucously through the countryside, I was lost in thought, dreading what awaited me at the end of the line. It was the decade of the 1950s, the years of the idealized housewife, the Korean War, and the launching of Elvis. As the king of rock and roll rocketed into our clean cut, apple pie lives, a less note-worthy event was occurring. Like flocks of birds, privileged graduates of private schools, such as myself, were migrating east to college. I'd decided to major in art and chose to attend Skidmore in upstate New York, a college known for its art department.

The Christmas holiday of my freshman year found me on the Knickerbocker, rumbling doggedly through the countryside on tracks snaking south-westward from Albany, New York towards Union Station in St. Louis, Missouri. Returning home to the Midwest filled me with gut-wrenching feelings. Being away had helped me to emotionally anesthetize myself to my parents' divorce, conveniently arranged to take place while I was gone. Now, however, I was coming face to face with reality. My mother no longer lived in the comfortable, lovely home in which I had been raised. Dad had moved into an apartment. Sadness, anxiety, and fear of the unknown engulfed me as I faced going home to a place that really wasn't "home." I thought about Mom living in a smaller house in Clayton with only my younger brother for company. And Dad, alone. The expectations of seeing them in strange, unfamiliar surroundings and my needing to split my time between my parents put an icy pall over my Christmas holiday. I'd be staying with Mom, but what about Dad? How was I going to adjust to visiting him in an apartment, a place that didn't seem to fit the dad I knew? Even though our family had its problems, at least we had been whole (or so I thought). Now we were fractured, seemingly out of control.

Mom had tried to make home as welcoming as possible. As she stood at the door and greeted me, a splash of bright colors over the fireplace grabbed my attention. Entering her living room, I couldn't imagine what those colors were. Then I remembered! They belonged to an oil painting I had done years before. In the squared, lined style of Mondrian, the painting was a gift to my mother, and she had decorated her living room around it. My eyes told me the message of her heart. She wanted me to feel welcomed, secure, and valued, yet I didn't. Although I experienced her welcome, I did not feel secure or valued. Deep in the recesses of my being I was afraid and felt worthless and ugly. For years, these crippling feelings, based on erroneous perceptions of myself, kept me from seeing the truth I know today. Now I know my worth, but then I couldn't see it because of the lies that were blocking the way.

The lies (negative feelings) began when I was a child, growing up in a home where there was little interaction between my parents. Though he loved us, Dad made his work his priority, and Mom was left raising three children alone much of the time. She was British and homesick for her native England, her family, and childhood friends. With a faraway look in her eyes, she would softly sing "The White Cliffs of Dover," and the longing in her voice for her beloved homeland confused me. Caught up in his world of finance, Dad didn't grasp the role of husband the way he did bread winner, and he was oblivious to her unhappiness. Communication between them was minimal, a fact that affected the whole family. We lived as islands, not sharing thoughts or feelings. I felt lost and unimportant, as if anything I had to say mattered to no one. The unspoken message as I heard it was: pretend. Don't let anyone know what's really going on inside.

This belief set the tone for my life. Self-deprecating thoughts festered in my mind. As a student, I was mediocre and emotionally walled in. Each brick in my self-protecting armor was a negative thought about myself. Socially, I was a misfit, more comfortable with rejection than acceptance. As the years went by, I sought professional help but to no avail. Although I had the opportunity to marry, I couldn't take the plunge. I reasoned there had to be something wrong with anyone who wanted to marry me, including the man I loved. So I ran from the relationship.

Running was a way of life. I couldn't bear to stop and look at myself. In the fall of 1973, feeling lost and without direction, I began to sink in a pool of hopelessness. As the murky waters were closing over me, I looked up and saw caring and acceptance in the eyes of a friend who was herself going through difficult times. I also saw peace in those eyes, and I asked her about the source of her peace, considering the difficulties she was undergoing. She told me about Jesus. She said what I saw in her eyes was Him, and that's the first time I realized there really might be a God. My thinking was turned upside down as my previously closed mind opened to the possibility of God's existence. A few months later, I was asked if I wanted Jesus in my life, and I said yes. My friend's caring had opened the door to an adventure that would affect the rest of my life. It was no longer mine to try to control. I still carried baggage, but now I had hope.

Years later that hope bore fruit when I went to a conference at the International Center for Biblical Counseling in Sioux City, Iowa. There, I attended a seminar that taught me about the healing voice of Jesus. I learned that bad experiences from my past are not responsible for my problems. Rather, the real culprits are *lies* I came to believe about myself as a result of the bad experiences.

Lies gripped me. All my life I had walked hand in hand with enemies like fear, insecurity, and worthlessness, all feelings rooted in lies I believed. I began to meet with a prayer counselor. As I shared past experiences and the pain and my conclusions, she would lead me in prayer, asking God if my perceptions and conclusions were true. It was like instant replay, and I'd remember painful events in vivid detail but now the Lord showed me the real truth about the event. One by one, I was released from the lies and pain of my past.

Over time, as my prayer life developed, a communication opened up with Him I didn't know was possible. I learned who I *really* am, as some of the vignettes in this book will show you. God redeemed what was bad and turned it into something good and honoring to Him. He took the painful years of my life and used them as a launching pad to put me in a prayer ministry to the emotionally wounded.

There are many aspects to God's healing of the wounded. Forgiveness and repentance, for instance, are two examples. However, I have not attempted to cover all that it takes to be set free from our emotional wounds. I have chosen rather to focus on how God exposes His heart for healing as He brings truth to those of us who have been filled with lies. We expose lies to Him and He listens, and He exposes truth to us, and we listen. The ways God speaks are varied. One way is with words. Other ways include thoughts, visual images, sounds, or the overwhelming sense of His presence. No matter how God responds to prayers for healing, His voice is truth, freeing people from lies.

Some years ago at the church I was attending, I took a class led by a professional Christian counselor. He asked one of his clients to share with us the results of her counseling. Sharon, a woman in her mid-thirties, conservatively dressed in gray, walked to the front of the room. I was expecting a testimony about healing, and I waited in anticipation. However, what she said caught me off guard. Her message was as colorless as her dress! She told us that she was on less medication and had learned to *cope* with her fears after six years of therapy.

My mouth dropped open. Six years! And still *only coping*! Her unenthusiastic tone of voice said it all. (I wouldn't be excited either!) Sharon was believing lies. She thought there never would be real healing, but she was wrong. God wants to heal, and He wanted to heal her. Sharon could have been totally freed from her fears.

Dr. Ed Smith calls what happened to Sharon "tolerable recovery." He writes,

> "Tolerable recovery would be like Jesus saying to the lame beggar on the side of the road, 'Do you want to

> be healed?' The lame man might reply, 'Yes indeed, heal me.' Jesus might say, 'Then here my friend, put these braces on your legs and take my arm for support and come hobble along with me down to the Jerusalem Physical Therapy Center and in no time you will be walking all on your own. Now friend, you must understand, you may walk again but you will probably have a slight limp. You will never be able to run or dance and you may be required to wear these braces for the rest of your life. Come hobble along with me for you are healed, sort of.'"[i]

Like Sharon, many people live their lives thinking they are "sort of" healed. However, merely coping with fear is not being healed. Jesus never said He came to help us cope with damaging emotions. He came to *heal* them! He wants our minds freed from lies that cripple us. He *willingly* heals.

Healing is what this book is all about. I have seen people set free from all kinds of mistaken beliefs. Some have thought they were failures and others that they were without hope. All of us are damaged emotionally and, to some degree, need our hearts and minds healed by the truth. In Paul's letter to the New Testament church in Rome, he counsels us to have our minds renewed with truth so that we might live out God's perfect will for our lives.[ii] Jesus taught that it's the truth that sets us free.[iii]

God wants to communicate truth to us. Many wounded people don't know this. They don't know Jesus as the lie-destroyer. Truth is within reach, and God does speak to us personally. We don't have to jump through hoops to find truth nor do we have to spend gobs of money to have Him come to us.

In *Rekindled Flame,* Steve Fry writes about hearing from God:

> Many are suspicious of the idea that people can hear God personally. They have seen imbalances, excesses, even downright deception. They have seen people doing things "in the name of the Lord" that appear provocative or inappropriate.... But these fears needn't keep us from fully enjoying the still, small voice of God. The knowledge of the Bible acts as a safeguard against deception, a sieve through which we sift mental impressions.[iv]

Over the last six years I have had the opportunity to minister to many emotionally wounded women and children. When they brought their lies to God and then shared with me what His still, small voice was saying to them, I knew falsehoods had been destroyed. His voice is truth. His voice is authority. His voice is power. The Psalmist wrote that God's voice breaks the cedars of Lebanon. His voice strikes with flashes of lightening. His voice twists the oaks and strips the forest bare.[v] His voice demolishes lies as nothing else can.

If you are wounded, go to God with your hurts. Let Him speak to you. Let Him destroy the lies eating away at you. Let Him fill you with truth. Healing and hope will burst forth, and your life will be forever enriched.

The Bower

"Buster kicked Lassie," little Delores Sifford cried, tears streaming down her cheeks. Running frantically away from the neighborhood "bad" boy, Delores found safety in her mother's waiting arms. "Buster is mean, Mommy. I hate him," she sobbed. Delores was beside herself with anger and hurt.

"Now, Delores, it's not nice to talk like that," her mother countered. Later that day, they walked to Buster's house hand in hand, "so you can play with your good friend," Mrs. Sifford said. Ringing the doorbell, she added, "I expect you to play nicely with him."

Delores was angry, hurt, and confused. She unconsciously learned what her mother modeled. Delores denied her feelings and concluded nice girls keep their mouths shut. They do what they are told and don't say what they feel. Mrs. Sifford had unknowingly robbed her daughter of the ability to relate well to people. They took advantage of Delores because they knew she wouldn't verbally defend herself. This resulted in fear and a lack of confidence on Delores' part.

Years later, her maiden name now changed to Bauer, she realized she needed someone with whom she could talk and pray about feeling fearful and valueless. As she shared her pent up feelings with me, I questioned her youthful conclusion that nice girls should keep their mouths shut. In prayer, she took the memory of Buster, her mother, and the conclusions she had drawn. Delores sat on the chair across from me while we talked and prayed. Then she began to describe what she was seeing.

"There's this huge presence, like a semi-transparent shield, that comes between me and Buster," Delores said. "The presence is Jesus, and He protects me. I can say, 'You are mean and cruel' to Buster because he can't do anything to me. Jesus' presence is there. I don't have to pretend. I don't have to hide bad things. I can call evil what is evil. God's presence is powerful. He is changing my name from Delores Bauer to Delores Bower. He's saying 'I'm creating a bower for Delores, a hideaway, where she can live and find protection in Me.' Lush trees and greenery surround me. It's awesome!"

God gave new names to many people in the Bible. Their names were symbols of how He had changed their lives. For example, Jacob, son of Isaac, had his name changed to Israel because he struggled with God and overcame. Abram became Abraham because God ordained him to be a father of many nations. Delores Bauer became Delores Bower because God wanted to affirm the life-changing truth He gave her. He is her protector.

He is your protector, too. You don't have to deny your feelings when someone is thoughtless or cruel to you. God is there for you. Let Him destroy the lies that tell you otherwise. Those lies will poison your thoughts. Find someone with whom you can talk and pray. Let God speak truth to you.

> *Therefore let everyone who is godly pray to you while you may be found; surely when the mighty waters rise, they will not reach him. You are my hiding place; you will protect me from trouble and surround me with songs of deliverance* (Ps. 32:6-7).

The Hallelujah Chorus

Kara's father was an oil executive working in Saudi Arabia where she lived most of her childhood. Her physical characteristics, light hair, and fair skin, marked her as being from another culture. Saudi nationals often treated her as inferior because she was "different" from them, and she developed damaging attitudes about herself. Kara felt like a misfit. She hated being different. Feeling left out, she rebelled. In a culture which considered rebellion by a girl unacceptable, Kara brought embarrassment to her family. By the time she was ten, her mother had labeled her daughter "hopeless."

As an adult, Kara now sat across from me and lamented, "I'm hopelessness personified." Gently challenging her belief of herself I said, "Let's pray and ask the Lord if you see yourself correctly." Willing to do so, Kara prayed and within minutes memories from her childhood in Saudi Arabia surfaced. Her shoulders slumped, and she covered her face with her hands. Hopelessness overwhelmed her. Then her hands fell away from her face. It was radiant. I could tell she was concentrating on something so I sat silent and waited expectantly. After a few minutes she whispered, "I heard the Hallelujah Chorus! Jesus is telling me He will take me all the way to victory over hopelessness, and there will be lots of Hallelujahs!"

Kara was experiencing intimacy with Jesus. In his book, *The Three Mary's*, A. Moody Stewart wrote:

> People "seek a distant Christ and reject Christ present. Jesus is near them, before them, with them; he is speaking to them in his word, he is listening to their prayer. And they are running to the ends of the earth in quest of him; turning from him where he is,

to seek him where he is not. He is not distant; and if they could reach the distance where they fancy him to be, they should not find him there, for he is not to be found except where he is."[vi]

Do you ever feel hopeless? If so, Jesus is present and available to help you. He is not a distant Christ, uninterested in your hurts. Right where you are make the decision to trust Him. Tell Him, "I will trust you with the care of my wounded heart." As Kara did, let Jesus destroy the lies ruining your life and replace them with hope.

May the God of hope fill you with all joy and peace as you trust in him, so that you may overflow with hope by the power of the Holy Spirit (Rom. 15:13).

Is Your Cup Empty?

Have you ever wondered why some answers take so long to come? Does it seem that you have been carrying a certain problem around forever? Have you about given up on ever getting it solved? A wedding feast in Cana provides an insightful look at why answers don't always come when we expect them.

Jesus, His mother, and His disciples are all at the feast. When the celebrants run out of wine, Mary turns to Jesus and says, "Son, they don't have any more wine. Please do something." But Jesus replies, "Woman, what have I to do with thee? Mine hour is not yet come."

Though Christ's answer to His mother seems disrespectful, it was not. Culturally speaking, it was an appropriate way of saying, "Mother, I can't do what you're asking. It's not my time yet." This was in keeping with Christ's commitment to do only what His Father wanted Him to do.[vii]

Shortly after this conversation, Jesus' hour came. That's when He changed water into wine for the wedding guests. Indeed, this was "the hour" for His show of power. But what caused Jesus to at first say that His hour had not yet come?

David Wilkerson, pastor and best-selling author, says he believes it was because the people at the wedding still had wine in their cups when Mary first spoke to Him. In effect, Christ was saying, "My time for demonstrating my power hasn't arrived because these people haven't yet run completely out of their resources. My hour comes when there's no hope—no remaining resources to depend on in the flesh. It is a moment of total dependence on me. And right now, for me to demonstrate my power, every container has to be empty. Dry. There can be nothing left in a single cup. All resources have to be exhausted. Then I can be a provider for these people. [viii]

The same thing is true today. More often than not people have to come to the end of their ropes before they turn to God. All tangible and emotional resources must be spent. Delores is an example. During the previous year she had gone to a psychologist who listened while she talked about her pain but gave her no feedback. She also visited a psychiatrist who put her on two antidepressants. Medicated, with no resolution of her problems in sight, she was desperate for help. That's when I met her.

As we talked Delores told me she was full of fear and shame. She felt she had to pacify people or they wouldn't like her. Sometimes she was even afraid they would physically harm her if she did anything to displease them. I suggested she ask God for a memory that would pinpoint the origin of her problem.

Settling back in her chair, Delores sat quietly and prayed. She let her thoughts drift back in time. Then she said, "In the first grade I had a teacher, Mrs. Morrison, who was mean. Once she punished me by putting me in a storage closet. I was so afraid and ashamed that I cried for days. After that, I felt I had to please her or she would put me in the closet again."

"Ask Jesus if it's true that you have to pacify people in order to keep from being hurt or feeling ashamed," I said.

After a few prayerful moments Delores replied, "I see scissors. God is cutting weights off me. They are lies I've been carrying around since childhood, keeping me from living free of shame and self-doubt. The weight about pleasing people is ugly. God is taking these weights off the six-year-old child so she can skip, run, and dance through life with Him. He is naming my feet Hope and Joy. That's what I'm to stand on."

Delores smiled.

How about you? Do you have hope and joy or are you weighed down with discouragement, your resources for the healing of an old wound exhausted? Have you tried all that the world has to offer and found that your cup is still empty? Dry? Are you longing to have it filled? Jesus can do that! He will fill it with healing truth. Will you let Him?

> *May the God of hope fill you with all joy and peace as you trust in him, so that you may overflow with hope by the power of the Holy Spirit* (Rom. 15:13).

Chapter 2

Desert Places

A Voice in the Desert

My trip to the Sahara was a desert experience in more ways than one. While I traveled in the desert physically, emotionally and spiritually I staggered through a desert of another sort. I wandered, following one mirage after another, lost, not knowing where I was going with my life. A recurring thought whirled through my mind. I imagined a half-dead leaf floating down from a tree, landing wherever the wind willed. The "leaf" was me. It never occurred to me that a caring God would pick me up out of the desert, breathe new life into me, and give me purpose and direction.

Late one night as I lay awake in my sleeping bag under a starless sky, I was reflecting on my misery. Surrounded by limitless miles of sand and rocks, this was no man's land as far as I was concerned. It was a geologist's dream, but I was not a geologist. For me it was a place barren of joy, companionship, and revelation.

"What in the world am I doing here?" I groaned.

As I lay there, tossing and turning, an unfamiliar whisper from the deepest recesses of my being penetrated my thinking and said, "When this trip is over, leave Chicago and return to St. Louis." In milliseconds I went from feeling lost and confused to having direction. I had vowed years before I would never return to my hometown to live, and the hold that belief had on me was instantly broken. I didn't understand where the whisper came from, but I was going to do what it said. That quiet voice had done something my family had lovingly, but unsuccessfully, tried to get me to do for many years.

I got up the next morning confident of my decision to return to St. Louis. I also knew I could survive the next two weeks in the desert. Now I had direction. I was going to make a major change in my life, and I was excited about it.

Back in St. Louis that fall, a friend invited me to a Billy Graham crusade. Though I was reluctant to go, I finally said yes and set out to be an observer. Little did I know that God had an entirely different agenda in mind for me. As Dr. Graham talked, I sat transfixed, face to face with the realization I'd made a mess of my life. What pierced my heart, though, was not hopelessness but hope. It filled the atmosphere, and I decided to trust what Dr. Graham was saying. Handing the reins of my runaway existence over to God, I knew He would do a better job of running my life than I had.

Some months afterwards, a friend sent me a news clipping in which Dr. Graham explained why he chose St. Louis for his crusade. He said that the Holy Spirit had specifically directed him to make this choice. I remembered the whispered voice in the desert that shattered the lie keeping me in Chicago. All of a sudden I understood the working of God's Spirit as I never had. He got me away from the distractions of my life in Chicago and into the barren emptiness of the desert so I could "hear" His quiet voice. God cared so much for me that He gave me a desert experience to bring me into His family.

I've since learned God often leads us into desert experiences. Moses found this out. Brought up in an Egyptian palace, he was used to the finest living quarters, the best food, the most elegant clothes, and power. However, he had a problem. His heart beat with Hebrew blood, but living in the luxuries of his adoptive Egyptian family, he couldn't relate to his beloved people. They were shepherds and slaves of their Egyptian captors. He couldn't stand seeing them helpless, beaten by slave masters day after day. He wanted to do something, but a huge gap existed between his life experiences and theirs. Acting impulsively, Moses took matters into his own hands and killed an Egyptian he saw beating a Hebrew.

Then Moses had to flee the country for his life. As a powerless fugitive Moses believed there was no way he could ever help his people. Instead of helping he had actually made their situation worse. Heading to the desert, feeling defeated, he herded sheep for 40 years before God showed up in a burning bush, telling Moses to go back and lead his people out of Egypt. After much coaxing, Moses was willing to do what God said. What Moses previously thought impossible was not.

A voice in the desert changed his beliefs, just as a voice in the desert changed mine. God still speaks to people today just as He did thousands of years ago. If you are in a desert place, it could be preparation for an encounter with Him. Do you have some beliefs about yourself you think are set in concrete? In reality those beliefs may not be true. Get prepared to let God show you the truth.

The voice of the Lord shakes the desert (Ps. 29:8).

Chapter 3

God's Hand

The Hand of Protection

Delores knew there was something lurking in her background that needed to be uncovered. She had feelings about herself she didn't understand. When her mother finally told Delores that she had attempted to abort her, Delores figured she knew where many of her self-deprecating thoughts originated. She was full of fear, afraid of being discarded by those who were supposed to care for her. She was insecure around people, even family and friends. Now she understood that these feelings began before she was even born.

Knowing the origins of the fear helped her understand why she felt the way she did, but knowledge by itself didn't heal her emotional wounds. "There's a reason for my fear," she said. "I picked it up in the womb because my mother attempted to get rid of me. This fear has nothing to do with what's going on around me right now. It's totally different than necessary fear, the kind needed for self-preservation." Delores continued to explain, "I can remember once driving a tractor. I lost control, and it spun around. I was terrified. That fear made sense because it involved what was going on right then and there," she said. "It was necessary."

"So," I asked, "Are you saying your fear of being discarded doesn't make any sense?" She agreed that it didn't. Still, the fear was real, and she needed deliverance from it. Intellectual understanding was good, but it didn't heal her emotions. Only God's Word could do that.

Asking God to intervene, we prayed for supernatural light to overcome the fear that shadowed Delores' heart. For a moment she sat quiet, head bowed, and hands clasped. Then she lifted her head, wide-eyed with amazement, and said, "I see a baby. It's me. There is a hand covering me so that nothing can get through. God is protecting me. He says, 'Your mother may forsake you, but I never will. Wherever you are I'll be there with you.'"

At that moment Delores realized God's hand had been there all along protecting her. She knew then she was not disposable. Absorbing this truth, she relaxed against the chair,feeling safe and wanted for the first time .

Are you fearful, feeling you might be tossed away by someone? Does your fear make sense or is it a lie, conceived in some dark place? Don't try to hide your insecurity. Lies dwell in hidden places. Talk to God. Tell Him the specifics about what troubles you. Ask Him for truth. He will liberate you and protect you with His Word.

> *...God has said, "Never will I leave you; never will I forsake you." So we say with confidence, "The Lord is my helper; I will not be afraid. What can man do to me?"* (Heb. 13:5-6)

A Bird in Hand

I was away for the weekend on a retreat with two friends. We were in the country on a farm, laughing, praying, and enjoying one another. Without thinking I began to compare myself to my friends. They seemed so full of the Spirit I was afraid I couldn't keep up with them. After all, they might leave me behind, choking in the dust from a spiritual getaway. Before I knew what was happening, fear and insecurity overtook me.

To escape from my feelings I went to bed early. I made a mental note to question God about what happened first thing in the morning. After a restless night's sleep, I got up and approached Him. I knew my thought about not being able to keep up with my friends was a lie. I asked the Lord for memories, and He brought to mind youthful encounters where I came away believing I couldn't keep up with my peers. Realizing this fear was a lie I still believed and lived by, I asked God to show me the truth. He proceeded to do so in a picturesque way.

I saw the Lord holding in His hand a bird, which I knew represented me. Sometimes His hand completely closed around the bird, and it was safe and secure. Other times, His hand opened up and the bird would fly away. At one point it fell and had the breath knocked out of it, whereupon it struggled and flew lamely back to God's hand. God healed the wound and breathed new life into the bird. Then He quoted an old saying, "A bird in the hand is worth two in the bush."

One person in God's hand has extreme worth. I knew His hand would always be there for me and I was in a place of safety and security, nestled in His palm. There would be no problem keeping up with my friends. God had replaced a lie with the truth, and I felt like a new person, full of value and energy, ready to enjoy the rest of the weekend.

God's Hand

Do you ever feel insecure for seemingly no reason? Are you afraid you can't keep up with the people around you? If so, perhaps your thoughts are recitals of lies you picked up in your youth. Stop struggling. Lie safely back in God's hand, and let Him heal your wounds. Let Him breathe truth into you.

> *If the Lord delights in a man's way, he makes his steps firm; though he stumble, he will not fall, for the Lord upholds him with his hand* (Ps. 37:23-24).

Chapter 4

Tearing Down Walls

Washed by Tears

A stone in the Wailing Wall in Jerusalem is creating interest for the international media. In July 2002, the 10 x 40 cm area in the ancient wall was damp when viewed from the front and glistening when viewed from the side. The general presumption by the media was that a pipe had burst or an old cistern had ruptured within the Temple Mount. Both were reasonable sounding solutions, given the extensive digging carried out by Palestinians within that area. However, Orthodox Jews see more than a broken pipe in the phenomenon. These Jews talk of ancient traditions which speak of the wall "beginning to weep" before the coming of Messiah.[ix]

Walls are noteworthy for different reasons. Sometimes they give protection as did the Wailing Wall at one time; other times they hold things back. For these reasons, people often create walls for themselves. People like Rebekah. She had built an emotional wall around herself. It held back tears threatening to erupt because of a terrible event that had happened to her. She believed she had to appear strong. After all, she was certain if a crack appeared in her wall, her tears might create a flood, causing her wall to collapse. Then everyone would know something was wrong. Her wall protected her, or so she thought. She hid behind it so people couldn't find out how much she hated herself. Sometimes people would try to knock the wall down, but she wouldn't let them get very far. She didn't want them to see who she really was. She believed as long as she stayed behind her wall, she would remain safe, hidden in the dark.

Eventually, though, Rebekah knew she needed light. Her life was going nowhere. She was stuck behind her wall. One day as we talked she began to remove bricks from her self-made protection and expose herself. As tears spilled from her eyes, her phony protection began to crumble. "I know I need to face the truth," she sobbed hysterically. "I can't live in denial anymore. I can no longer hide from the ultimate betrayal." She gathered up her courage and with garbled words said, "My brother raped me." Trembling, her body contorted in agony, she continued, "He was like a tiger on top of me, devouring me. He...he pawed me. I couldn't stop him. I was only six."

Since that terrible crime, Rebekah had felt helpless. Nothing mattered. "I'm disgusting," she groaned emphatically. "As far as I'm concerned, God's deserted me. I'm too dirty."

"The God I know wouldn't leave you," I reassured her. "I understand why you feel angry and helpless and dirty. But, Rebekah, those thoughts and feelings are lies. If you will bring them to God, He will take them and give you truth." Curled up on her side in the chair, arms hugging her pain to herself, she said, "Are you there for me, God? Or have you abandoned me? I really want to know the truth." Then she waited. Silent.

In a short time I heard her say, "Jesus says He loves me. A big tear from heaven is falling on me. He grieved when I grieved. What happened to me was nothing He intended. I'm being washed by His tears. It's as if all the poison that's been in me since I was six, is being washed away. I feel detoxified."

Cleansed, Rebekah was wrapped in peace.

Have you built a wall around yourself because you have suffered at the hands of someone? Have you sought safety by emotionally shutting yourself off from people? If so, walls aren't the answer. Let God remove the poisons in your thinking that made you believe you had to build that wall. Then it will start crumbling. Be honest with God. You have the choice of feeling the pain for a moment or living with it for a lifetime. He has not deserted you, and you are not too far gone to be helped. God will bring you healing and cleansing truth, detoxifying you from your lies.

> *Those who sow in tears will reap with songs of joy* (Ps. 126: 5)

Overcoming Walls and Barriers

In the spring of 1999 I was vacationing with friends in Puerta Vallarta, Mexico. While there, we accepted an invitation to a party in a condo overlooking the harbor. On the appointed evening, we parked our car on top of a mountain that encircled the city and walked to the condo's front door, stepping down steep steps carved out of the mount's stone. Once in the condo, I expected to be in an enclosure. Surprisingly, though, I found myself still outside. Grasping for my bearings, I suddenly realized I was in an "outdoor living room." Feeling as if I was in another dimension of time and space, I stood staring at the limitless expanse before me and the stunning, brilliant blue ocean waters below. This home, tucked into the side of the mountain, had no exterior wall on the front and only a partial wall on one side. Standing in the living room, I gazed out at the unending space. Talk about awe-inspiring! Now, however, when I think of that place, I don't think of its beauty. I think of the absence of walls and barriers.

Though some walls can be good, many walls that we create for ourselves are rooted in our own wrong conclusions about someone or something we have experienced. I remember Carla, a dental assistant. She emotionally isolated herself behind walls and barriers. When Carla was ten years old, her father abandoned the family. Like many children do, she blamed herself for his leaving, believing that he would have stayed if she had pleased him more.

She also reasoned that since she couldn't keep her father around, she would never be able to keep a husband. After all, if her dad found her unlovable, no one else could love her. Carla further concluded, "There has to be something wrong with anyone who would love me." These were the lies by which she lived. She built walls to protect herself from hurt which kept her from getting close to people. These walls caused problems in her relationships with her husband, family, friends, and God.

Carla wept as she shared her feelings and the beliefs fueling them. Then as we prayed and asked Jesus if her beliefs were valid, the pain engulfing Carla seemed to melt away almost immediately. I witnessed the change in her countenance as God brought her out from behind the barrier which had long blocked her emotional growth: "Jesus says He loves me," she said, wiping her tear-stained eyes. "If there is something wrong with someone who loves me, that means there has to be something wrong with Jesus, and I know that's not true."

Like Carla, do you have walls and barriers keeping you from giving and receiving love? Maybe you feel there has to be something wrong with someone who would love you. If so, don't let this lie keep ruining your ability to enjoy your relationships to the fullest. Let God take that lie and destroy it with truth.

> *The unfolding of your words gives light; it gives understanding to the simple. I open my mouth and pant, longing for your commands* (Ps. 119:130-131).

Turning Pain Into a Pearl

When we embrace pain, as Jesus did, and decide to face it for the sake of His name, we share in the rewards which go along with that decision. Properly embraced, pain opens the door for us to have an intimate relationship with God. Bob Sorge writes:

> The Scriptures use the pearl as a brilliant example of this truth. Pearl is the natural substance an oyster produces when it is afflicted from an outside source. When a gritty grain of sand settles into a crevice inside an oyster's shell, located in such a way that the oyster cannot dislodge it through its natural means of squirting out water, the oyster has a backup system for dealing with the irritant. It secretes a substance that produces a soft, smooth coating around the grain of sand—a substance called pearl. Over time, layer upon layer is added. Eventually, that which vexed and pained the oyster is the very thing, which produces something of great value and beauty.[x]

Pain and vexation filled Delores childhood. She remembered getting spankings for falling in a mud puddle or for playing with her little friend next door without permission. If she cried after being paddled, her mother would spank her again. The worst fear gripped her when her mom would threaten to put her in a girls' home. Delores lived in a state of fear. To protect herself, she put up an emotional wall behind which she hid herself and her feelings. No one could get to her behind her wall of fear. She also found another means of escape—her bedroom closet. The darkness would wrap itself around her, befriending her. Delores would sit there, listening intently to every little sound, terrified her mother would find her.

Forty years later, Delores still lived in a closet, one of her own making. Struggling to get the words out, she told me about the fear and pain that haunted her life. Eager to grow in her relationship with God, she hoped He had answers that would change her view of herself. In a soft voice, forcing words to come forth, she said, "I feel like trash, dirty, something people just want to throw away. I hate myself. Hiding is a way of life for me." Asking God to take her mind back to the source of her feelings about herself, she leaned back against the chair, expectantly waiting.

Soon she said, "In my spirit I see myself as a child hiding, crouched down in the closet. Jesus is opening the door. The bright light around Him is overcoming the darkness. He's reaching in to take hold of me, pulling me up towards Him. He's smiling. I don't have to be afraid. He's showing me I don't need a protective barrier around me anymore. It kept me safe as a child, but I don't need the barrier. It feels like a cage to me now.

"Jesus keeps talking to me. Like a hammer, His words are shattering the walls of my cage. He's telling me that when the apostle Peter was in a trance he saw heaven open and something like a large sheet let down to earth by its four corners. It contained all kinds of four-footed animals, reptiles and birds. Peter was horrified. He called the animals unclean. That's how I feel about myself! Yucky! Unclean! But God told Peter not to call unclean anything that God has made clean. That includes me! God created me. He doesn't make trash! It's arrogance to go against His word!"

We talked a bit, and a new thought brought a smile to Delores' face. She said, "It's like the oyster covering the irritating grain of sand with a coat of pearl. God's Word covered my feelings about myself with a layer of truth." Then as she brought more lies to Him, He continued to cover each one with truth. Layer after layer of truth obliterated the irritating lies.

Do you feel "yucky" and unclean, as if you have to hide from life? If so, let God speak pearls of wisdom to you just as He did to Delores. He will replace your negative feelings about yourself with truth and make those feelings into pearls of great value. God is just as alive today as He was when He let the apostle Peter see heaven open. With words of truth, God will open heaven for you, too.

Do not call anything impure that God has made clean (Acts 10:15).

God's Acceptance

Interesting insights come to families when they research their genealogies. This is as true for the family of God as it is for biological families. In the first chapter of Matthew, there are four women, in addition to Mary, the mother of Christ, who appear in His genealogy. In Jewish tradition, it was not customary to list the names of women, and there is an interesting possibility as to why Matthew chose to do so.

One of the women in Matthew's list was named Tamar. She was Judah's daughter-in-law. Because she had tricked her father-in-law into having sex with her, she doesn't seem to be the type of person you would expect to find included in the ancestry of Jesus Christ. Neither does Rahab, a prostitute. Next Matthew mentions Ruth, a Moabitess, who is automatically of questionable character. Finally, Matthew lists Bathsheba who was coerced by David into an adulterous relationship.

It is comforting to know there were women in Jesus' genealogy who didn't have picture-perfect lives. Most of us haven't had that kind of life either. Realizing Jesus accepts us, warts and all, makes us feel more kinship with Him. Could it be that Matthew lists these women because he knew we could identify with them in some way? Is it to show us Jesus accepts us unconditionally regardless of our background or life choices?

Donna certainly didn't have a picture-perfect life. Twice divorced, full of fear and anxiety, she struggled in life. As a two year old, she was in the hospital with pneumonia for a month. The nuns scared her because they always seemed to have needles in their hands. The seemingly never-ending penicillin shots caused little Donna to see people as overpowering and hurtful. Her unconscious defense was a wall of fear. As an adult, that wall was still present. She was shy, unassertive, always letting people walk over her. Donna grew so used to the wall's presence she didn't even know it was there until we talked one day. When she finally saw it, she was convinced she still needed the wall. "People will hurt me without it," she said. I suggested we pray and ask Jesus what He thought.

Turning her attention to Him, she prayed for the truth and then told me what she saw: "Jesus is making a hole in the wall. It's made out of paper with a wood frame. He's coming through the hole, making funny faces at me, picking me up and holding me on His shoulder. I'm safe."

Donna smiled, feeling relieved and accepted, the fear gone.

Maybe you are someone who can identify with Tamar, Rahab, Ruth, Bathsheba, or Donna. Maybe you've made choices so bad you think God will never accept you or affirm you. If so, you are wrong. Find someone to pray with you. Let God speak truth into your spirit, demolishing lies that have been holding you back from really living. Once the lies are replaced with truth, you will be changed.

> *You were taught, with regard to your former way of life, to put off your old self, which is being corrupted by its deceitful desires; to be made new in the attitude of your minds; and to put on the new self, created to be like God in true righteousness and holiness* (Gal. 4:22-24).

Chapter 5

By Whom Do You Measure Yourself?

Removing the Mask

One Friday evening, I sat intently listening as Lynn Feinberg, leader of a congregation of Messianic Jews and Gentiles in St. Louis County, spoke about hostility toward Jews. She traced anti-Semitism back to its roots.

Historically, anti-Semitism began with Jacob and Esau, brothers of Jewish parents. Esau, the oldest son, gave up his inheritance when he traded his birthright for a pot of stew that his younger brother, Jacob, had cooked. In keeping with the same offhand attitude toward his Jewish heritage, Esau married a pagan woman and through his lineage, a grandson, Amalek, was born. The Amalekites, his descendants, were the first people to attack the Israelites when they fled Egypt and entered the wilderness.

The Germans, one of the people groups descended from the Amalekites, continued generational anti-Semitism leading to the Holocaust in the 20th century when millions of Jews went to their death under the Nazi regime. The spirit of Amalek controlled the Nazis and lives on even now, thousands of years after Amalek's death.

Generational attitudes are as true for individuals as they are for people groups. Barbara's life is an example. As most children do, she grew up emulating her mother. Self-controlled, her mom rarely showed emotion. Barbara never remembered hearing her mom cry or show fear, so she concluded her mom didn't want anyone to know her thoughts or feelings. Barbara became the same way, believing it wasn't acceptable to admit to having her emotions. In an effort to hide her feelings, Barbara became somewhat of an actress.

"My mother called me Sarah Bernhardt," Barbara recalled in a sarcastic tone of voice. "I control and manipulate by my actions, instead of dealing with people in a straightforward way, because I don't want anyone to know what I'm really feeling. It's as if I'm on a boat in a strong current with no oars," Barbara said, her voice faltering.

Shaking and desperately needy, she asked God to take her back to the origin of her fear of being real. As she sat there, her eyes opened wide as a memory from her childhood surfaced. "I see my mom standing by the kitchen door and my father, suitcase in hand, getting ready to leave forever. Mom is silent, cold, like a rock, determined not to show any emotion. I was about three years old and scared, but I wanted to be like mom. I wouldn't dare let on how I really felt."

Her eyes brimming with tears, Barbara told God she was tired of acting and didn't want to hide from the truth of her own feelings anymore. She pleaded for help and then quietly waited for a response. She soon relayed to me the picture God gave her.

"I'm at a masquerade party. I see someone with a mask on. All of a sudden the mask flips off revealing the real person behind it. It's me! The mask is off! I can be me!"

Can you be who God created you to be, or like the people groups descending from the Amalekites, have you maintained a negative generational disposition that causes you to act in ungodly ways toward others? There are many people who are of a different social status, faith, educational level or gender than you are. Can you be vulnerable and admit to yourself how you really feel about them? Or maybe, like Barbara, you've acquired a hurtful attitude that makes you feel you have to hide your true feelings. If so, chances are you are wearing a mask and living a lie. Ask God to take you back to the origin of that lie and replace it with truth.

. . . *the truth will set you free* (Jn. 8:32).

Your Value

One particular Sunday afternoon, I sat curled up in my favorite chair, commiserating with myself, my mind running out of control. Having no children of my own, I bemoaned my empty arms and thought of a little girl I recently held. I missed her. I missed having a child to fuss over. I felt sorry for myself.

I was miserable. Slowly, however, I started to come to my senses. The desire of my heart is to have my identity in God. Many women find their identity through their husbands or children. Having neither puts me at a disadvantage, some think. However, I don't see it that way. The more I let God take over my life, the more secure I feel, the more my identity blossoms. It's a process, though. The problem is, there are parts of me, such as being childless, that I give over to God and then take back. That's when my pity parties become a problem. Lies come to the forefront and obscure the truth.

The simple truth is that God loves me. He loves me uniquely and personally. He guides me through life as a Father would his child. He gives me grace and mercy, even when I don't deserve it. Under His hand, there is more of Him in me and less of my old self. He has taken me from being a directionless, unhappy woman running from life to being a woman who feels complete and fulfilled in Him.

Despite all these blessings, however, my mind wandered to an undesirable place on that Sunday afternoon. I had mentally ventured into a nest of vermin, spitting out old lies, "You don't measure up; you're a nobody, a loser." Mentally I knew these words weren't true, but my heart was telling me otherwise. I asked God if there was any truth coming from these harassing creatures.

First the Lord gave me a memory from which these lies

originated. Softly speaking into my spirit He said, "Rejoice in the 'child' you have given birth to—the St. Louis Pregnancy Resource Center.* Your breasts have given nourishing 'milk' to needy women. Your arms have held newborn babies and given love to the lonely. You are an integral part of a growing family. You are a spiritual mom in the fullest sense." Overwhelmed with God's love, I was transformed from feeling sorry for myself to being thankful for who I am.

What a loving God we have! He reminded me that I had started a ministry to women faced with unplanned pregnancies. It was birthed from a clear word He had spoken into my spirit. Passionately believing God created life and that every person, born and unborn, is important to Him, God let me be "mom" to the St. Louis PRC. Babies now live because their mothers decide not to abort them and choose life for them. Counseling at the center helps women through hard choices and difficult times. The Center's Bible studies give "milk" to new Christians, nourishing and encouraging them. And the post-abortion ministry to hurting women brings God's love and forgiveness.

God was showing me my value doesn't come from letting old lies continue to live in me. My value comes from letting Jesus fill me with truth from His Word. Life with Him is an adventure. The more I fill myself with His truths, the more valuable I feel.

Do you feel as if you don't measure up? Are you wallowing in self-pity, believing old lies spit out by a nest of vermin? If so, let our awesome God fill you with truth.

**I founded the Pregnancy Resource Center in 1983. It was a birth experience taking nine months from the time God conceived the idea in my mind until we opened the doors of the first office.*

Nothing is a greater faith builder than seeing Him show you your value.

> *Sing, O barren woman, you who never bore a child; burst into song, shout for joy, you who were never in labor; because more are the children of the desolate woman than of her who has a husband* (Isa. 54:1).

Touching Jesus' Hem

Olivia filled the doorway as she entered my living room. Stopping to size up the the furniture to see which piece would hold her huge frame, she chose the sofa, walked over to it, and fell back onto the soft cushions, her breath coming in short gasps. As she talked with me, it became apparent that of the cast of characters involved on the stage of her life, her Italian mama played the most prominent part.

Olivia's mother held high expectations for her child, starting at an early age. Measuring up to these expectations, however, was beyond little Olivia's ability. Scornfully, her mother would say, "Olivia, you'll never measure up to me." So wanting to please her mother, Olivia felt defeated in all but one area. Eating. She would stuff herself with everything her mother prepared. A cook from the old country, her mother's food was heavy with starch and fat. Her mama loved to cook, and she loved to eat. Her size bore testimony to both. She would say, "Olivia, you'll have to eat more potatoes than that to keep up with me!" Olivia did. She grew bigger and bigger, becoming more and more like her mother. Her mother was Olivia's measuring stick.

Thirty years later Olivia was suffering the consequences of being not only an overeater but also a people pleaser, feeling she felt she had to please everyone. I told her to pray and God would show her if this desire to please was based on a lie or God's truth.

As she trusted Him, He took her back to memories of her mother saying, "You'll never measure up to me." Feeling the pain of those biting words, she asked God if they were true.

She soon told me what she heard in her spirit: "God is saying that if I have someone I try to measure up to, that's idol worship. He has a different image of me than my mother had, and He doesn't make demands on me. He says, 'My yoke is easy; My burden light.' The belief I've had that I don't measure up unless I please people is a lie. That belief is heavy, not light. I shouldn't be carrying it. God's idea is to have me walk and talk with Him each day. Knowing, listening, and obeying Him is what makes me measure up."

The scriptures tell of a woman who had been rejected so much she didn't feel she measured up either. Hemorrhaging for twelve years, she was an outcast, considered to be unclean and untouchable. People, including family members, could not lie on the ailing woman's bed or sit where she sat. In those days there was little tolerance for a woman with this kind of ailment.

Jesus didn't treat this woman as if she were an untouchable, though. When she managed to get through the crowd around Him and touch the hem of His garment, He spoke right to her and said, "Daughter, your faith has healed you. Go in peace."[xi] In Jesus' day it was usual to address the opposite sex as "woman," and normally that is what He would have said. But in this case, Jesus did not call her "woman" for a very specific reason. He wanted her to be both physically and emotionally made whole. He did this by publicly calling her "daughter," a loving title that included her in His family, giving her worth and emotional healing.

Jesus is speaking healing words today, just as He did in biblical times. Are you weighed down with lies telling you that you don't measure up, that you have to please everyone? Whatever your problem is, push ahead. Humble yourself. Go and touch the hem of Jesus' garment by getting alone with Him or praying with someone. He will give you a healing word just as He did for both Olivia and the hemorrhaging woman.

Then Jesus said to her, "Daughter, your faith has healed you. God in peace" (Luke 8:48).

You Are a Gift

Children who are abused don't appreciate their value. They are so focused on just surviving they fail to see beauty either in themselves or in their surroundings. Erica was one of these people. Cruelly treated as a child, she never learned to appreciate the loveliness of a flower or the smile on a neighbor's face, let alone her own beauty. All she could think about was getting through each day unharmed.

This survivalist mentality continued on into adulthood, even though Erica's abusers were not present in her adult life. Erica often visited me in my home, and the loveliness of my backyard began to have an impact on her. She spent hours enjoying the sight of the cardinals, chickadees, titmice, and woodpeckers frequenting the bird feeders. Her interest in birds began to blossom. For the first time, she began to really see these lovely creatures as her eyes opened to the beauty around her.

One day we noticed the sparrows had multiplied rapidly and were taking over the birdhouses, chasing away previous inhabitants. I did some research and discovered these aggressive tree sparrows were considered to be of no value. Their population increase has rendered them a nuisance, and in Missouri it is even legal to shoot them.

Yet Jesus had some interesting words to say about sparrows. He said His eye is on them and that "not one will fall to the ground apart from the will of your Father." Maybe Jesus singled out sparrows, considered to be the "least of these," to teach us a lesson. Does He want to show us that He cares about those whom others see as worthless? After all, if He cares that much for sparrows, how much more does He care for us?

Erica didn't know how much God valued her. From day one her earthly father let it be known she wasn't welcome in his family because he wanted a son. All her life he took out his bitterness on his daughter, which made Erica feel unwanted and unloved. While these feelings were true in her relationship with her father, it was not accurate to believe everyone else felt that same way about her. This latter belief was the lie destroying Erica. She took her feelings to Jesus, the One who is truth Himself. Then she told me what she saw and heard in her spirit.

"Jesus is there. I see Him right by me at my birth. I feel safe. He is smiling and happy I'm me. Dad is angry I'm born. He's disappointed, but Jesus isn't. He's not angry that I'm who I am. He says I'm a gift."

Hope appeared in Erica's eyes.

Do you know you are a gift to someone? Do you know you have value or do you think you are unwanted and unloved, perhaps even a nuisance like the tree sparrow? Erica had a lot of lies to overcome. As she brought each one to Jesus, He filled her mind with truth, and her feelings about herself changed. Build your identity on who Jesus says you are, not on the words of someone who spoke lies to you.

> *Are not two sparrows sold for a penny? Yet not one of them will fall to the ground apart from the will of your father. And even the very hairs of your head are all numbered. So don't be afraid; you are worth more than many sparrows* (Mt. 10:29-31).

In Whom Is Your Worth?

Karen's mother was burdened. Cooking, cleaning, and caring for her four children, she drove herself, seemingly striving for perfection and supermom status. Caught up in her busyness, she didn't take the time to cuddle or play with Karen. Reading to her or just enjoying Karen's company was out of the question. Because she was the oldest, Karen was enlisted to take care of her baby brother. If she performed well as her brother's keeper, her mother would compliment her. This compliment became the only praise Karen got from her mom. Karen grew up thinking her worth came from what she did, not from who she was.

As Karen grew older, she married and had children of her own. Besides being a wife and mother, she also was a registered nurse, taking care of patients in the local hospital. From all appearances she looked as if she had it all together. She didn't, though. Karen was a defeated Christian, wearing a superficial smile, and still working very hard to get enough praise to feel significant.

As we prayed, God gave Karen memories of all the work she did to try and please her mom. "All my life I've felt if I perform my duties well, I would feel worthwhile. Is something wrong with this philosophy? Life isn't working out the way I thought it would. Why do I feel so unappreciated, empty, and worthless?" Sharing her frustration with God, she waited for an encouraging word.

God's encouragement came in the form of a picture. Karen described it to me: "I see myself as a little girl in Jesus' lap. He's holding me and comforting me." She smiled. "I have never experienced such love. Nor have I ever felt so special. I don't have to do anything but receive. I don't have to prove myself. Jesus accepts me just as I am." Her eyes sparkled. "This is a whole new concept for me."

Believing performance is necessary for worth has been a problem for people down through the centuries. The Pharisees of Jesus' day were performance-oriented. Like Karen, they focused on working hard and getting rewarded. They did not comprehend, nor want to believe, they could not earn God's favor but only receive it as a gift. They studied the scriptures, yet they didn't even recognize Jesus, the One spoken of in the very words they diligently poured over, when He was right in front of them. Their desire to perform blinded them.

Like the Pharisees, are you blind to the truth, feeling you have to perform to be acceptable? Like Karen, do you feel unappreciated, empty, and worthless, even though you have worked long and hard? If so, you don't know God's unconditional love and acceptance. You don't know your worth comes from who you are, one of God's special, one-of-a-kind creations—not from what you do. Bring your negative feelings about yourself to God. Let your mind drift back to a memory where these feelings were conceived, and then ask Him if what you believe is true. Let Him introduce you to the real value you are to Him.

> *For it is by grace you have been saved, through faith—and this not from yourselves, it is the gift of God—not by works, so that no one can boast* (Eph. 2:8-9).

The Gold Room

"My socks don't match," lamented Melody. She was remembering an incident that happened to her when she was eight years old. Little Melody attended a birthday party, and she felt she didn't fit in with the other girls who looked so happy and pretty. Melody thought she was ugly and a misfit. When she happened to look down and see her mismatched socks, she was sure her thoughts about herself were true. Now, a woman in her twenties, she was seated on my sofa, talking about an incident she had not thought of since her childhood. The feelings Melody had about herself then were the feelings she had about herself today.

The adult Melody could have blamed the memory of her childish discomfort on the mismatched socks she wore to that birthday party. She realized, though, that the mismatched socks were only a manifestation of something deeper going on inside of her. Then she remembered that on the way over to the party, her parents had had yet another fight. As children often do, little Melody so identified with the yucky dysfunctional fighting in her family that she herself felt she was yucky.

Years later, still feeling like an ugly misfit, Melody sought help. She brought her feelings about herself to the Lord, desperately wanting to be free from her mental shackles. Slumping forward, hands clasped, she asked God to show her the truth.

After a short period of silence she said, "In my spirit I see a big room with my feelings about myself in it. The room shrinks and turns into an ugly little brown box. Now the scene changes and the box is in a shiny, gold room. I'm there dressed in a plain white gown, not fancy. The Lord is there, too, and says, 'Lies were all the ugly brown box ever contained. Its power doesn't compare to the truth anymore than the ugly box compares to the beautiful room. Now the box is a pile of ashes, burnt up. The room feels safe. There's lots of light and white and gold. I want to stay."

Melody was beginning to discover who she really is. God was showing her that her lies didn't match the truth any more than her socks matched each other.

Do you ever feel "yucky," as if you're a misfit? If so, do you think this matches the way God feels about you? You are wrong if you do. The solution is not "thinking outside the box" but discarding it entirely. God wants to burn up the ugly box of lies that has been keeping you from feeling acceptable. Let Him impart truth to you. He wants to heal you so that you might be confident and take part in all He desires for you.

> *I have no greater joy than to hear that my children are walking in the truth* (3 Jn. 4.)

The Hedge Trimmer

The phone rang. "Is this Carrie?" a vaguely familiar voice questioned. "Yes," she answered. "This is your Dad." There was a pause. "I know it's been 25 years, but ah...what I mean is...." His words hit Carrie like a knife in the stomach, and stunned beyond belief, she felt herself spiraling backwards to her childhood of abuse. Repeatedly she had been shamefully used by her dad and other members of her family. Now as an adult, she had sought help for three years in a Victims of Sexual Abuse support group. Her emotional problems improved ... until the phone call. Now all the horrible lies that victims of sexual abuse believe about themselves came tumbling forth: "I'm unattractive, powerless, a dirty dishrag." My heart went out to her as she shared her confusion and anxiety with me. She said she felt Jesus had fed her to the wolves. I suggested the first thing we should do is to ask Him if, indeed, this was so.

Carrie agreed. Bent over in the chair, with her hands covering her eyes, she asked Jesus in a despairing voice if her thoughts about His abandonment were true. After a few moments, she proceeded to tell me what He was showing her. He gave her a picture of vines all over her body. These vines both gripped and paralyzed her with tentacles that wove their way into all areas of her life, even undisciplined places like finances and eating. She said, "One stem is my grandmom, one is my dad, one is my mom, one my grandpa, and one is the refrigerator. The shoots coming off the bigger stems are my peers. Their grip on me began 31 years ago. Not just my body, but my whole life is tangled up.

"Now there's this old man, dressed in a hat and overalls, with a wheelbarrow full of tools. He moves slowly, and he loves his job. He's kind and walks over to me.

"'What are you doing?' he asks.

"'I'm picking at the vine, but little pieces just grow back. I'm trying to get untangled, but it's growing so fast I'm not getting anywhere.'

"He replies, 'What you are doing isn't working because it's been growing for 31 years. I know a better way.' I'm thinking he's going to help me pick away at it, but instead he took out a big hedge trimmer. The sun reflects off the blade, and it was really sharp. He bends down to the ground where I can't reach and takes the first thick stalk and cuts it. On that vine at the base is the word, 'Grandmom.' The lies, heartache and pain from her abuse dry up. With the next stalk—and the next and the next and the next—he does the same thing. He cuts them at the base.

"Now the parts of the vine that wrapped and bruised me are relaxing. I can see where they were. All the pieces are starting to shrivel and release their grip on my body. When he's done, I have bruises, a rash, and places where the vine wounded me. He goes to the wheelbarrow for salve and puts it on me. I feel pain start to leave. He gathers up his tools, steps out of his overalls, and I see He is the Lord."

Do you see who God really is or do you believe He has "fed you to the wolves?" If you believe the latter, you are entangled in lies. Let God release you from the grip of those lies, as He did Carrie. Let Him take His hedge trimmer and chop off your dreadful perceptions at their roots. Let Him give you memories that pinpoint the origin of your lies. Let Him breathe truth into you. Truth is a healing salve that will bring freedom and joy into your life.

> *They have greatly oppressed me from my youth—let Israel say—they have greatly oppressed me from my youth, but they have not gained the victory over me. Plowmen have plowed my back and made their*

furrows long. But the Lord is righteous; he has cut me free from the cords of the wicked (Ps. 129:1-4).

A Good Samaritan

Opal Brown gave birth to her daughter, Paula, in a home for wayward girls in the 1950s. To cover up her daughter's illegitimacy, Opal told Paula her father was killed in a freak accident while serving in the military. A few years later Opal married, but her husband didn't want little Paula around. Opal took her to visit her grandmother, and without a word of explanation, Opal left her daughter there. Paula was crushed! She grew up feeling totally abandoned and unlovable.

Deeply wounded, her little heart was broken. It was still in pieces when I met her as an adult. Paula sorely needed God's healing. Sitting in my living room, looking down at the floor, she said, "I feel like dirt." I told her if she would take that thought to Jesus, He would show her if what she felt about herself was true.

"After all, He is the truth and can't tell you anything but the truth," I said. She agreed to try.

Sitting stiffly, she closed her eyes. After a few seconds she told me what she saw: "Jesus says, 'Let Me tell you what I've done with dirt. I made mankind out of it and I used it to heal the eyes of the blind man.' Jesus is reaching out to me. He's motioning me to come to Him. He's telling me how important I am." Absorbing these words of love and healing, she smiled and sat peacefully back in the chair.

There is an individual spoken of in the New Testament who must have felt like dirt. He was a victim, robbed, stripped, and beaten, left to die on the road between Jericho and Jerusalem. The first man who found him was a priest. Seeing the victim, the priest moved to the other side of the road. Maybe he was coming from a religious service and anxious to return home. It's apparent he *wasn't* anxious to get involved. The second man to approach the victim was a

Levite, a respected caretaker, service provider, and associate priest in the tabernacle. It would have been more in character for him to stop and minister to the victim, but he didn't. He passed on, too.

Finally, a traveling Samaritan found the victim. When he saw the wounded man, lying on the ground, the Samaritan took pity on him. He bandaged his wounds, pouring on oil and wine. Then he put him on his donkey and took the victim to an inn. Paying the innkeeper to look after the victim, he said he would reimburse him for any extra expenses when he returned.

Paula felt like the victim. Like a Good Samaritan, Jesus came along and ministered to her. He bandaged the first of many wounds, pouring on the oil of the Holy Spirit and the wine, His own blood. Then He paid the price for her with His death on the cross. And, finally, He carried her to a place of rest in Him.

Are you a victim? Do you feel like dirt at times? Give Jesus the chance to show you His love. Let Him be a Good Samaritan to you and bandage your wounds with truth. It will lead you to a place of rest. Lies won't. They only bring misery, not peace.

And the words of the Lord are flawless, like silver refined in a furnace of clay, purified seven times (Ps. 12:6).

Wearing Today

A painting hanging over the fireplace of the Francis Schaeffer Institute in St. Louis County caught my attention. Part of a collection of acrylics and prints displayed at the Institute, this painting's message caused me to stop and think. On its left side, the artist painted a copy of a dramatic work by nineteenth century artist, Francesco Goya, "The 3rd of May, 1808: The Execution of the Defenders of Madrid." In it is a group of six men, all their bodies except one distorted in fear. Some are on the ground, curled up on their sides with their knees drawn to their chests in terror. The one exception, a Spaniard in a brilliant white shirt, is in stark contrast to the dark surroundings. He stands boldly, arms outstretched, in a crucifixion-like stance. On the right side of the painting is a close-up rendering of a twenty-first century figure, a cherub-faced-boy of about 12, facing the viewer. With his back turned to the group, a smirk on his face, and his right arm extended behind him, the boy's right hand holds a gun pointed at the men. *That boy represents what's happening in America today to a certain segment of our youth,* I thought sadly to myself. *He wants to shoot God, and he doesn't see people as human beings, only as "things" in his way.*

A "thing"! That's how Dallas saw herself. As a child, she felt like a millstone around her mother's neck, standing in the way of her mother living a good life. For example, whenever Dallas did anything wrong, her mom would look her in the eye and say, "I'd like to *shoot* you." Although said only halfheartedly, her words were a lethal weapon. In retrospect, Dallas felt her mother really meant what she said. Dallas had long ago concluded she couldn't do anything right.

She told me about a hurtful incident when she was five

years old. She was proud of herself because she had worked hard to learn her ABCs. Yet when she got the chance to say them to her mother, she was scared because she was afraid to make a mistake. She really wanted to do a good job to please her mother. She did great until she got to LMNOP, and then she had a memory block. Mimicking her mother, in a disgusted, nagging voice, Dallas crudely paraphrased her mom's words to her those many years before: "You can't do anything! I work my butt off, and this is what I get!" Dallas had been crushed.

She grew up believing she was responsible for her mother's misery. She felt she was a burden not only to her divorced, unhappy mom but to everyone else as well. When I told her that her thoughts about herself were lies, her eyes widened in anticipation and curiosity. She was eager to go to the Lord to have Him deliver her from this hurt.

She closed her eyes to pray, asking for truth, and as the light of understanding dawned, she told me the insight God gave her. "It's summer, and Jesus is taking off a heavy wool coat I'm wearing. He smiles and puts a silky garment on me. 'This is what you need,' He says. 'You were wearing something out of season from the past. Today this garment is what you need to be wearing. It's from Me—light, not heavy. You've been wearing that outdated coat from your past.'"

Have you been carrying a burden on your back? A burden you took on when someone spoke lies to you? Maybe that person made you feel like a "thing," just something in the way. Maybe your life is distorted with fearful thoughts such as "people would like to *shoot* me." If so, go to the Lord with those lies and ask Him to show you their origin. Then ask for truth. It enables you to stand boldly, knowing who you *really* are.

Come to me, all you who are weary and burdened, and I will give you rest. Take my yoke upon you and learn from me, for I am gentle and humble in heart, and you will find rest for your souls. For my yoke is easy and my burden is light (Mt. 11:28-9).

Soaring or Scratching

There's a Native American story about a brave who found an eagle's egg and put it into the nest of a prairie chicken. The eaglet hatched with the brood of chicks and grew up with them.

All his life the changeling eagle, thinking he was a prairie chicken, did what the prairie chickens did. He scratched in the dirt for seeds and insects to eat. He clucked and cackled. And he flew in a brief thrashing of wings and flurry of feathers no more than a few feet off the ground. After all, that's how prairie chickens were supposed to fly!

Years passed, and the changeling eagle grew very old. One day he saw a magnificent bird far above him in the cloudless sky. Hanging with graceful majesty on the powerful wind currents, it soared with scarcely a beat of its strong golden wings.

"What a beautiful bird!" said the changeling eagle to his neighbor. "What is it?"

"That's an eagle—the chief of the birds," the neighbor clucked. "But don't give it a second thought. You could never be like him."

So the changeling eagle never gave it another thought. And it died thinking it was a prairie chicken.[xi]

Caroline had a "prairie chicken" image of herself. She had never ever entertained the thought that she could soar on an eagle's wings. Brought up by a mom who never encouraged her, Caroline thought she would spend her life scratching on the ground for life's leftovers. She was angry, felt unloved and of no value. Her mother's interest in other things superseded her interest in Caroline. "I'm not a

Tiffany vase or a bottle of booze," Caroline said sarcastically, in reference to her mother's value system.

Caroline was also angry at her grandfather. When she was a child, her mother would take her to visit Caroline's maternal grandparents in the summer. Mother and daughter shared the big bed in the guest room. At night, her drunken mother would fall asleep immediately, but there was no sleep for Caroline, only the beginning of a real live nightmare. Her grandfather would open the bedroom door, seek out Caroline, and molest her, while she was right next to her mother. When Caroline tried to tell her mother, she refused to believe her.

I could see anger overtaking Caroline as she told me this story. Her mother's denial caused her to feel as if her words were without value. "No one wants to hear what I have to say. I'm not worth anything," she said.

When I told Caroline God wanted her to get past the false conclusions she had drawn about herself, she was anxious to pray. Closing her eyes, she raised her face to the light and asked for truth.

Telling me what she heard in her spirit, she said, "I laid down my life for you. I am all you need. Your worthiness comes from Me. When you are lost, I look for you just as a shepherd looks for his sheep. I have the deepest love for you. Stop looking for affirmation from people. Your worth doesn't come from them. It comes from Me." Caroline, a lost lamb, received truth from her divine Protector.

Do you feel worthy, as if you could soar like the eagle? Or are you feeling like a prairie chicken? If you answer yes to the latter, scratching around on the ground has caused you to ingest a lie. Somewhere along the way you've drawn wrong conclusions about yourself. Ask Jesus to show you the truth. Then meditate on it. Swallow it. Let it change you.

> *Do not work for food that spoils, but for food that endures to eternal life, which the Son of Man will give you* (John 6:27).

Chapter 6

Light on Earth

A Star Is Part of a Galaxy

When Campbell was a child she always came home from school to an empty house. Though her mother was home physically, she "wasn't there" for Campbell emotionally. Her mother lived locked away in the prison of an unhappy marriage and used alcohol to deaden her pain. Her problems were so great she could not meet the needs of her little girl. Campbell's dad, it seemed, was always traveling on his job. Like all youngsters, the little girl needed reassurance and affirmation. Emotionally unprotected by her parents, the door was open for Campbell to see herself in the wrong way. While it was true her parents were not available, her belief that no one would *ever* be there for her was not true. This belief, based on wrong conclusions from her family experiences, was a lie by which she lived.

The affect of this lie was devastating. As an adult, Campbell ran her own life and trusted no one. Nothing could change her belief that she had to live her life alone until, at age 30, she became a Christian. Then she found herself in a struggle—on the one hand believing what the Bible said about being a part of God's family, but on the other hand, deep in her heart, still believing no one really cared about her.

Confused, she came for prayer. As we talked, Campbell admitted she felt isolated. She said, "I've always felt there was no one there for me, yet the scriptures tell me otherwise. They say I'm part of the body of Christ. Jesus is the head, and we are His feet, arms, and hands. We are to need each other. Yet I don't feel as if I'm there for anyone, and I don't feel anyone is there for me. Why don't my thoughts line up with what scripture says?" We prayed and God gave Campbell memories of coming home from school to an "empty" house. That repeated experience had caused her to conclude, "No one will ever be there for me. I have to live life alone."

In compassion and wisdom, the Lord whispered truth to her: "You are a lovely star, but a star is part of a galaxy. If a star shines alone, it will not light up the night. It needs an array of other stars with it to bring light to the darkness. You are out there all alone, and no one can see your light. You need others to be effective." Campbell's eyes were opened. Now she knew the truth and could take the first step to come out of her cocoon-like existence.

Are your eyes open to the truth or to lies? Are you a star with a light no one can see or are you part of a galaxy? If you are running your own life and living apart from the body of Christ, your light is most assuredly dim. You need truth or the darkness will overwhelm you.

Just as each one of us has one body with many parts, and these parts do not all have the same function, so in Christ we who are many form one body, and each part belongs to all the others (Rom. 12:4-5).

The Morning Star

Recently, after a ministry session that did not go well, I found myself flooded with feelings of inadequacy. My mind started to play an old tape which said, "You won't make it. You're going to fail." God has done great healing in me, destroying lies, but that doesn't mean new ones don't occasionally surface. When they do, I generally recognize them immediately. Now I knew it was time for another round of truth. I asked God to help me remember the first time I felt inadequate. Within moments, a memory surfaced, and I was reliving the original event. Then I asked Him, "Is this true? Am I really inadequate?" In my spirit He spoke, "You are my bright morning star. Light flows from you and illumines the dark places in people."

At first I questioned whether or not these thoughts were really from God because I'm not the morning star. The Scriptures are quite clear that Jesus is.[xiii] Then, as I waited before Him, He showed me something else. A morning star appears just before dawn when the night is coldest and darkest. I have risen before dawn for years in order to spend the prime hours of my day with Jesus, basking in the warmth and light of His Word. And now I realized He was affirming my actions. He was patting me on the back, letting me know I really am a morning star. I began to see there's no inadequacy in that! If we will bring our darkest, coldest lies to Jesus, along with the memories where the lies were conceived, He will beam His bright light on them, destroying the lies with truth.

Do you need the bright light of the Morning Star to illumine a dark place in your life? Is there a lie telling you failure is just around the corner? Boldly seek God. Ask Him for truth to light up your darkness. He wants you to be a star.

You, O Lord, keep my lamp burning; my God turns my darkness into light. With your help I can advance against a troop; with my God I can scale a wall (Ps. 18:28-29).

Chapter 7

The Light From God's Jewels

Black Diamond

One of my great winter joys is a blazing fire in the fireplace. The fire's differing intensities of light and color enliven my spirit. The other night I sat mesmerized in thought, engulfed by the warmth and atmosphere of the leaping flames, when suddenly I became aware there was nothing but darkness. The flames had disappeared, hiding themselves in the coals. I waited, wondering if the fire would re-ignite itself. As I sat and watched, I began to realize that sometimes the truth about ourselves is like the flames of that fire. It gets hidden behind the blackness of lies.

Then I thought of Kelly. A past of neglect, rejection, and rebellion left her believing she was hopeless. Intellectually she knew it wasn't true, but negative messages written on her heart at an early age told her otherwise. Her heart overruled her intellect. I told Kelly the way to free herself from feeling hopeless was to ask God to show her the truth. He would rewrite the script on her heart.

Kelly hung her head and wept. Covering her face with her hands, she told God about her pain and hopelessness. Then she asked Him if what she believed was true. She waited. In a few moments she began relating what God was speaking.

He said, "I'm examining the trash of your past life, piece by piece, holding it up to the light. The pieces are like coal. You can't see through them. They are black, opaque. Yet the longer I look at each piece, the more I see. There are nicks, scratches, and lots of hurt, but I like these pieces of coal. I can see their potential. They are different from the clear, crystal-like pieces some people give Me to examine. Your pieces are to be handled. The more I handle them, the shinier they get, like black diamonds."

Kelly smiled, a look of remembrance in her eyes. She told me that years ago, while on vacation in Mexico, she had bought a silver bracelet. In its center, surrounded by a nest of silver leaves, was—you guessed it—a black diamond!

Feeling as if she was in the center of God's presence, Kelly was surrounded with peace.

Does the fire in your heart need re-igniting? If it does, take a few minutes right now and tell God, like Kelly did, about the hurts and disappointments from your past that make you feel hopeless. Wait quietly before Him and listen to what He says. He will take the dull, black coal of your life, polish it with His love, and make it into a black diamond.

And we know that in all things God works for the good of those who love him, who have been called according to his purpose (Rom. 8:28).

From Prison to Prism

I had gone to the Arlington Hotel in Hot Springs, Arkansas, to join family for Thanksgiving. As it turned out, I wasn't feeling well. Not wanting sickness to keep me from enjoying my family's company, I sought out the whirlpool in the hotel's spa, hoping to sweat out my viral intruder. Covered in the water's heat, I was asking God to use it to draw unwanted toxins from my body. As I was thinking about my physical health, I remembered times God had applied heat to restore my mental health.

More than once He had put me in hot water to deal with my toxic thinking, which poisoned my belief system, just as germs poison my body. I recalled times I thought I was a nobody until Jesus showed me I am a somebody.

Wanting out of my confining mental prison, I had asked Him to overcome my feelings of being a nonentity. I desperately wanted my life changed. In a quiet voice, He spoke words to my spirit that lifted me into a realm where I could move forward, out from behind the steel bars confining me: "You are not in prison but in a prism. This prism reflects light because I am light. It's blinding! Go into the prisons! Go into the darkest places and bring my light."

The lie had such a hold on me I couldn't see who I really am. But I know now that I'm not a nobody; I'm a light bearer. Not only did I find truth and affirmation, I received confirmation about God's call on my life. Through prayer and ministry I am to go into the darkest places of peoples' hearts—where toxic thinking resides—and bring the light of Jesus. I am to help others find the truth I had found for myself.

Do you find yourself in hot water? Maybe God has you there to make you look at your toxic thinking, which keeps you in a confining mental prison and turns you into somebody you are not. If this is true of you, let Jesus' truth shine into the dark place where that thinking resides. Receive light that will detoxify your thinking so that you will know who you *really* are.

> *The Spirit of the sovereign Lord is on me, because the Lord has anointed me to preach good news to the poor. He has sent me to bind up the broken-hearted, to proclaim freedom for the captives and release from darkness for the prisoners* (Isa. 61:1).

Unconditional Love

Once upon a time there was a young girl named Susie. She was a beautiful little girl with the most wonderful doll collection in the world. Her father traveled all over the world on business, and he had brought dolls home to Susie for nearly 12 years . In her bedroom she had shelves of dolls from all over the United States and from every continent on earth. She had dolls that could sing and dance and do just about anything a doll could possibly do.

One day one of her father's business acquaintances came to visit. At dinner Susie took him by the hand and showed him these marvelous dolls from all over the world. He was very impressed. After he took the "grand tour" and was introduced to many of the beautiful dolls, he asked Susie, "With all these precious dolls, you must have one that is your favorite. Which one is it?"

Without a moment's hesitation, Susie went over to her old beat-up toy box and started pulling out toys. From the bottom of the box, she pulled out one of the most ragged dolls you have ever seen. There were only a few strands of hair left on the head. The clothing had long since disappeared. The doll was filthy from many years of play outside. One of the buttons for the eyes was hanging down with only a string to keep it connected. Stuffing was coming out at the elbows and knees. Susie handed the doll to the gentleman and said, "This doll is my favorite."

The man was shocked and asked, "Why is this doll your favorite when you have all these beautiful ones in your room?"

> She replied, "If I didn't love this doll, nobody would!"
>
> That single remark moved the businessman to tears. It was such a simple statement, yet so profound. The little girl loved her doll unconditionally. She loved the doll not for its beauty or abilities but simply because it was her very own doll.[xiv]

Kim felt the same way about Dolly. Kim had Dolly since childhood. Knowing this, I was deeply touched one day when, wanting to thank me for something, Kim asked me in a childlike voice, "Would you like to have my doll for a few days?" My mouth fell open and my eyes grew wide. Smiling in delight and surprise, I humbly accepted her treasure on loan.

Kim had gotten Dolly from her sister, Kathy, who had many dolls. One day, deciding she didn't want Dolly anymore, Kathy threw Dolly in the trash. Kim, who had neither dolls nor toys, retrieved Dolly. Kim would hold her close, talk to her and tell her things she never told anyone else. Kim would hide Dolly under her bed so that when her dad came in her room at night and did horrible things to her she never felt alone. Dolly was her sole and secret comfort, retrieved from her hiding place only when no one was around. Kim knew her dad would destroy Dolly if ever he found her, just as he had Kim's other playthings.

Except for Dolly, Kim grew up believing no one could love her. As an adult, she was aloof, acting out what she believed about herself. She had few friends and allowed her work to absorb most of her time. It was there, overhearing a colleague's conversation, that she heard about my ministry to emotionally wounded women and children. Knowing she needed healing, Kim made the decision to come for help.

Opening up about her terrible past, she shared with me one painful memory after another. We brought them to the Lord, along with the lies she believed about herself. With each lie God spoke truth and healing into her wounded psyche. When she expressed being unlovable, He said, "You *are* loved by Me. I am your Father. Your soul was exterminated by your birth father. You died. There was no you, only a shell. However, I came along, nurtured you, and brought you out of darkness. I resurrected you. You are fully alive now, precious and cherished."

Do you ever feel unlovable, as if no one could really care for you? Kim thought no one but her doll could do that. Some people think only their pets can really love them. Her Father in heaven showed Kim she believed a lie. Do you? If so, let God bring you out of darkness into the light with His truth.

> *The people walking in darkness have seen a great light; on those living in the land of the shadow of death a light has dawned* (Isa. 9:2).

Chapter 8

Getting Unstuck From the Muck of Your Beliefs

Dissolving Sin Into Smoke

"Breaking Faith" the headlines read. A Baptist minister, pastoring a church in Detroit, was one of three church leaders accused of sexual abuse by members of his congregation. Admitting his guilt he said, "I failed the Lord, I failed my congregation, I failed the people involved, I failed my wife, I failed my children; I sinned against them."[xv] This humbled pastor, no doubt, knows he is forgiven. Nevertheless, he is still vulnerable to the enemy's accusations. He could allow his sense of guilt to override what Jesus Christ did on the cross.

In his book, *I Am,* Steve Fry writes,

> "Satan knows this, of course, and that's why he seeks to accuse us at every turn. His very name, 'the accuser,' reveals what is perhaps his primary tactic against us as he strives to keep us off balance in our relationship with the Father. Always pointing a finger, he tries to wear us down until we are reduced to shadowboxing our discouragement."[xvi]

Recently, Sarah was being worn down by flashbacks of sexual sins she committed before becoming a Christian. She knew that Jesus had taken those sins when He was on the cross, but it was easier to see that for others than for herself. Every time memories of past sins were triggered, she was devastated. She felt like a hypocrite when she called herself a Christian. She was convinced that if people really knew what she had done, they wouldn't want anything to do with her. It seemed as if the accuser was pointing his finger at her, trying to keep her from seeing the reality of God's forgiveness. Believing that He would bring truth, she asked Him to fill her with it and blot out the lies of her accuser.

Telling me of God's response in her spirit, she said: "Jesus is painting smoke over my sins. I can't see them anymore. It's like they never happened. They've disappeared, just like smoke does."

Is the accuser trying to wear you down? He is a liar, a thief, and there is no good thing in him. Let Jesus smoke out the finger pointer's charges and give you a fresh infusion of truth.

> *Therefore, there is now no condemnation for those who are in Christ Jesus* (Rom. 8:1).

Feelings

"Children should be seen and not heard." Believing this childhood mantra caused Becky many problems. She never talked about her fears or feelings of rejection because she was taught that "Children should be seen and not heard." Like most small children, she suffered the usual childhood agony of being called "names." But she didn't tell her mother and get the usual hugs and loving words of reassurance she needed. When some of her little neighborhood friends called her "Becky-icky-goo," Becky suffered alone. Ashamed and afraid, she hid her crushed feelings, believing the lie of her childhood.

The summer Becky was 12, she attended Camp White Bark in California. While there, she went to great lengths to hide her unhappiness. Every Saturday night 40 campers squeezed themselves into one of the cabins for "feast night." Girls happily joked and told stories to one another during a frenzy of eating junk food and drinking soda. Afraid her fear of being rejected might be exposed, Becky hid her feelings behind a wall of potato chips, coke, pretzels, and cake. She gorged herself, and every Sunday she would be violently sick. The gorging enabled her to hide her feelings from herself and those around her.

As an adult, Becky still did not talk openly. Unable to express herself well, she was angry and withdrawn. We talked and prayed. A memory surfaced of her mother saying, "Children should be seen and not heard." On the conscious level, Becky had never been aware of the terrible effect these words had upon her. The lie that resulted from them, though, was imploding inside of her. Her unconscious belief that "I should not express my thoughts and feelings" was choking her, snuffing out expression, leaving unwanted debris.

After asking God for cleansing truth, she sat quietly. Within moments, I could see her intently listening to His reply in her spirit. Repeating it to me, she said, "I made you to feel and have emotions. I am emotional. When My people were in a sorry state, I wept over them. Let go of your control and express your emotions. Emulate Me. Weep with those who weep. Rejoice with those who rejoice. Express the full gamut of feelings I have given you."

Is a lie keeping you from expressing the full range of your God-given feelings? Are you able to express love? Are you able to weep with those who weep and rejoice with those who rejoice? Becky hid behind a wall of junk food to hide her feelings. Are you hiding behind something that keeps you from expressing your feelings? Food? Drink? Being the group clown? TV? If so, ask God to give you a heart that wants what is hidden brought into the light. Then seek help from someone who will pray and minister to you, asking for God's truth to destroy the lie inside you.

> *When Mary reached the place where Jesus was and saw him, she fell at his feet and said, "Lord, if you had been here, my brother would not have died." When Jesus saw her weeping, and the Jews who had come along with her also weeping, he was deeply moved in spirit and troubled. "Where have you laid (Lazarus)?" he asked. "Come and see, Lord," they replied. Jesus wept. Then the Jews said, "See how he loved him!"* (Jn. 11:32-36)

Our Watchman

At the tomb of Jesus, Mary Magdalene turned around and saw Jesus standing there, but she did not realize that it was Jesus. 'Woman' He said, 'why are you crying? Who is it you are looking for?' Thinking He was the gardener, she said, 'Sir, if you have carried Him away, tell me where you have put Him, and I will get Him.' Jesus said to her, 'Mary.' She turned toward Him and cried out in Aramaic, 'Rabboni!'[xvii]

Jesus was standing right in front of Mary, yet she did not recognize Him. She was looking for His crucified corpse, not her Lord in the flesh.

Mary's thinking is typical of the church today. Too often we're more comfortable with Jesus' corpse than with His living being. Don't most people today speak of religion, a belief system rewarding behavior rather than relationship? Isn't a reward system more sought after than a real connectedness with the living God?

Erica was a struggling musician who wanted to be connected with God but was blocked by a belief that affected both her growth in Him and other ambitions as well. She believed that no one would want her. She was afraid that she would fail both in her relationship with God and her desire to play the guitar semi-professionally.

One day I received the following note from her. She wasted no time in getting to her point: "Mary, I flashed back to something that happened to me when I was a child. I earned money and bought a cheap guitar. My dad said I could play it only when he was gone but no more! One time I told my brother I wanted to be like Glen Campbell and play my guitar. He told my parents. That night dad came storming into my room. He yelled a lot, punished me, hit me, slapped and laughed at me. He said he would see to it that I would never say such foolishness again. The next day I came home from school and my guitar was gone. My dad, I guess, sold it. We never talked about it again."

Never talking about it again gave the enemy an opportunity to plant lies in Erica's mind. She believed she was going to fail in her attempts to be a musician. "I'm foolish to think I can succeed; no one will want me," she often said, pinpointing a lie needing God's light.

Finally, tired of being stuck in the muck of her beliefs, Erica prayed and asked Jesus if her father's actions had led her to form wrong perceptions of herself and her abilities. Shortly, in the stillness of her spirit, she heard a few simple words. She softly repeated them to me: "I see Jesus. He says, 'Come.' He's holding His hand out to me. He wants me with Him. 'Trust Me,' He says. I'm taking His hand, and we're walking together."

With a peaceful look on her face, Erica rested, knowing that she was wanted! As lie after lie was destroyed, truth changed Erica. Today she is a sought after musician, playing for groups in the area where she lives.

Would you trust Jesus to take you by the hand and lead you to the truth? If not, maybe you are more comfortable with His corpse than with His life. Maybe you think there's no way He can change the way you feel about yourself. "Feeling unwanted is just a fact of life," you might bemoan. If this is your thinking, then you are caught in the snares of religion, not a relationship with the risen Savior.

Trust in the Lord with all your heart and lean not on your own understanding (Pr. 3:5).

Flying High

Nine-year-old Anthony had a soprano voice and loved singing in his school's choir. However, his high clear voice and love for music earned him the name "sissy." He was devastated when his schoolmates teased him and called him "mama's boy." Sometimes their voices would ricochet off the walls of the school as they tauntingly tormented him: "You're a girl, a girl, a girl...." These were lies, of course, but at his vulnerable age, Anthony was afraid they might be true.

He was still hurting when I met him a year later. Head drooping and feet dragging, he came with his mother for ministry. He told me he wondered whether or not he was really a boy. I suggested we go to the Lord and ask Him. Humped over in his chair, speaking in monosyllables, he prayed, and then remembered Mrs. Jamison, his music teacher, calling him a crybaby. Face downcast, eyes closed, he asked Jesus to tell him the truth. Was he really a sissy and a crybaby and a girl and all the other things the kids had called him? Then he sat silently. After a few minutes, his eyes popped open and a big smile crossed his face. He exclaimed, "I'm good at music! It hasn't made me a girl or a crybaby!"

What a contrast! So freed was he by God's simple revelation, he jumped up from the chair exclaiming, "My heart weighed 150 pounds when I came here. I felt like I was on a seesaw, and I was so heavy I couldn't move. Now my heart's so light the seesaw's throwing me up in the air!"

Do you have a heavy heart about something? Is a lie, possibly an epithet hurled your way, keeping you down? If so, it doesn't matter whether you're nine or ninety. Bring your feelings to God and tell Him you want to fly high with healing truth.

Let the little children come to me, and do not hinder them, for the kingdom of heaven belongs to such as these (Mt. 19:14).

Through the Valley

"When your call to be a compassionate healer gets mixed up with your need to be accepted, the people you want to heal will end up pulling you into their world and robbing you of your healing gift."[xviii]

Danielle, a divorced woman in her forties, suffers from a number of physical ailments. I discerned that her emotional wounds could possibly be a cause of her physical problems and conveyed this to her. She called for an appointment, and we had two sessions. Painful memories came forth, some lies were uncovered and God's truth was spoken. Shortly after our second meeting, she pulled me aside in a chance encounter and said she did not want our relationship to be ministry oriented. She wanted a friendship. Without thinking, I reluctantly agreed.

Later, though, in my spirit I knew she was attempting a distraction to avoid her pain. If I bought into her wish, I would have been pulled into her world, and we both would be robbed of the blessings God wanted to give us. She would not be freed from the pain of the lies she believed, and I would lose the blessing of ministering God's healing truths to her. I would have been a people pleaser, not a God pleaser. Unfortunately, I never got the opportunity to tell her my feelings, and we did not meet again.

Most people will do anything to avoid having to re-live a painful event. After all, don't we spend hours filling our lives with busyness, work, drugs or other things to avoid unpleasant realities? But pain won't go away. It won't resolve itself, and it might even manifest itself through physical ailments. While I understood the choice Danielle made, it grieved me. I felt sad knowing that other than praying for her, there was nothing more I could do.

When people let God take them back to a memory in order to gain truth, it can be akin to "walking through the valley of the shadow of death." They don't stay stuck in it. They go *through* it. They can't walk around it or avoid it. And once they get to the other side they find tremendous freedom.

Like Danielle, do you think the valley of the shadow of death is too dark to travel? Why? Maybe you believe you might get stuck in it. Do you realize your very reason is a lie itself? A lie which keeps you stuck? It's in the "presence of our enemies," such as fear and pain, that God promises to provide a banquet for us. That banquet is an abundance of truth and comfort.

> *Even though I walk through the valley of the shadow of death, I will fear no evil, for you are with me; your rod and your staff, they comfort me. You prepare a table before me in the presence of my enemies. You anoint my head with oil; my cup overflows* (Ps. 23:4-5).

Trashy Thoughts

My aunt grew up in Austria. Like most northern Europeans, littering was a habit she learned early to avoid. Last fall, 84-year-old Aunt Lorli and I were chattering away, strolling along a side street in Hot Springs, Arkansas. As we passed a deserted lot, pock-marked with debris, she muttered, "I hate trash." Her comment set me to thinking.

How many of us have trashy thoughts cluttering our minds? Joan did. As a 13-year-old, walking down the subway steps one day in New York City, she was accosted by a man who molested her. Another similar incident had occurred years before when her grandmother left her with an assumed friend. Until the day she sat in my living room, Joan had never told anyone about his mistreatment of her.

As she talked about these incidents, Joan told me she felt unclean, defiled, and at fault. She said, "I feel I have to hide from life. There's no safety, no one to watch out for me." Then she added, "I used to sing this poem: 'I'm alone and afraid in a world I haven't made.'"

"You haven't made the world," I agreed, "but there is One who has." The lot in Arkansas, littered with people's trash, suddenly came to mind, and I said, "Those men from your childhood dumped their trash on you. The debris left lies, and they are littering your mind. Let's go to the Creator, truth Himself, and ask Him to remove those lies."

Joan brought her memories of the abuse and the lies that permeated her mind to Jesus. Like others before her, she bowed her head, asked for truth, and waited. Then she said, "I see myself when I was thirteen. Jesus is kneeling so He can look me in the eye. He's talking with me. He's saying, 'You can tell me anything.'" She looked up then, and I saw the pain vanish from her face. "I feel cherished by Him. He's telling me He will always be with me and that He's my God, my shepherd, and my friend. He's telling me to come to Him and let Him give me rest." At peace, she leaned back and picked up her dulcimer, the instrument she carried with her every time she came for an appointment. Her lovely voice filling the room, she sang a song that clearly showed her feelings: "No One's Ever Cared for Me Like Jesus."

Do you feel that God cares for you or do you think He has made you to be "alone and afraid in a world you haven't made?" If you don't know He cares for you, your mind is littered with trashy thoughts. Give Jesus a chance to sweep those thoughts away and put His truth in their place.

> *Find rest, O my soul, in God alone; my hope comes from Him* (Ps. 62:5).

Affirmation From Our Father

Sidney, a single woman in her late 40s, is the daughter of a military father, a strict disciplinarian and perfectionist. The family had to "snap to attention" whenever her father was around. She remembers sitting at her desk in the first grade, crying and crying because she made a mistake. She was afraid Ms. Kretschmar, her teacher, would tell her father. Sidney thought he wanted her to be perfect and would punish her if she didn't live up to his standards. She lived under the constant fear of failure, disapproval, and punishment from her father.

Her dad traveled a lot, so Sidney and her sister often lived only with their mom. She, too, was afraid of her husband. When he was around, Sydney's mother was like a mindless, plastic robot. "She never stood up to dad," Sydney said. However, when he was gone, a metamorphosis would take place. She was her real self, carefree and attentive to Sidney and her sister. They did fun things together like making peanut butter cookies for the neighbors. In the winter they'd go sledding down the hill in the back yard. Sidney grew up thinking life was more fun without her father. She concluded men were to be feared. The thought of marriage was scary.

Our fathers play a great part in our lives. Their actions affect how we perceive ourselves as well as how we perceive other men. Henry Nouwen in his book, *The Only Necessary Thing*, says he believes the core moment in Jesus' life came at His baptism when His Father said to Him, "This is my beloved Son in whom I am well pleased."[xix]

God affirmed His Son. Sidney's father, however, never did affirm her. She didn't think she could ever please her dad. Her feelings toward him also influenced her attitude toward men in general. She didn't think she would ever be perfect enough to live up to their expectations. We prayed and asked Jesus to show her the truth.

After a long silence her eyes popped open, and she said, "I saw Jesus picking me up from my desk in the sixth grade, holding me, patting me, comforting me. He is proud of me, whether I make mistakes or not. I don't have to be perfect. There is nothing fearful about Him. He took me to Ms. Kretschmar, and she told me I don't have to be afraid."

Sidney saw that all her life she had believed a lie.

Have you been doing the same thing? Are you afraid of making mistakes and not being perfect? God is not a strict disciplinarian, expecting you to "snap to attention." Give Him a chance to show you how much He loves you. Let Him give you truth that will free you from the bondage of perfectionism.

> *Surely you desire truth in the inner parts; you teach me wisdom in the inmost place* (Ps. 51:6).

Putting Delores Back Together

One segment of "Sixty Minutes" on CBS featured 89-year-old Studs Terkel, who talked about his latest book on dying and death. It is a compilation of opinions from people about what happens when we die. When asked about his own death, he said that he wasn't sure, but he had noted that those who had faith were in the best position and seemed to have the most peace.

"Faith in what?" I thought to myself.

Delores had faith. The real thing. But she didn't know until she was middle aged how to put that faith to work to heal her wounded emotions. As a ten-year-old girl, she shut down emotionally after being molested by an uncle. She withdrew, living in her own world. When her uncle took advantage of her, it seemed her last shred of trust in people was destroyed. There were only two things she could count on—God and church.

Forty years later, strong in her faith but feeling emotionally weak, Delores came for ministry. Open to bringing her memories and beliefs about herself to God, He spoke truth. She relayed to me what she heard in her spirit: "It's as if I've been splintered into pieces. People have been able to take pieces of me for their own purposes. Jesus wants me to make a request of Him. He wants me to say, 'I want You to get those pieces and put me back together.' He's waiting for me to give Him the signal to do that. The only place the pieces are safe is with Him. I've been an emotional cripple all my life because people have taken too much from me, and I didn't know how to say no."

Delores prayed, giving Jesus the signal to mend her. In her spirit she saw Him put the pieces of her mind, emotions, and spirit back in place. She said, "I'm together again. There were emotional broken bones He mended, too. As literal broken bones grow back stronger than before if properly mended, the same is true for emotional bones too. I have new strength in God because emotionally broken bones have healed. I'm stronger than before. I feel complete."

Do you feel complete? Or have you let people take pieces of your mind, emotions, and spirit, leaving your personhood with holes of co-dependency? If so, give Jesus the signal to get those pieces back and plug up the holes. And how about your bones? If broken by tragedy, let God mend them with truth, making them stronger than before. As you walk in completeness, your faith in Him will be magnified in unimaginable ways.

> *For he has not despised or disdained the suffering of the afflicted one; he has not hidden his face from him but has listened to his cries for help* (Ps. 22:24).

Our Protector

I have a mental picture of my mother, comfortably seated in her upholstered, high-backed chair, darning our family's socks. I can see her, needle in hand, peacefully darning away, absorbed in her mending. She had a box of darning supplies, and whenever one of us got holes in our socks, out would come the box. Mother would go to work, doing what Grandma had done before her. Nowadays, I never see anyone darning socks. I suppose we think we don't have to do that anymore. We just go out and buy whatever new foot covering is being marketed that week. Things are so disposable, so easily replaced.

Cheryl felt that way—disposable, as if she could be easily replaced. She remembered being a ten-year-old child, feeling she was a bother. Her dad would plant himself in front of the TV, demanding silence. She liked to sit beside him, but if she talked, he would fly into one of his rages. Once he threw a cup at the wall, and she fled in tears to her room. Her dad escaped from his surroundings by watching TV. He didn't have to feel or deal with life or responsibility. Cheryl learned to do the same thing. She protected herself from her dad's rages by keeping quiet, numbing her feelings, and ignoring anything unpleasant. Her emotions were imprisoned by his rage.

As an adult, Cheryl recognized her need for help in dealing with her emotional problems. She said, "I'm a zombie. I don't feel what others feel. Most of the time I go numb in order to survive." I told her God would bring her truth if she would bring Him memories of her father and the lies she believed about herself. Quieting herself, she told God she felt like a prisoner, unable to express her emotions.

Shortly, she said, "I see a picture of Jesus standing between me and my father. Jesus is taking blows. They are not physical but verbal. Jesus is my protector. I can cling to Him, hiding behind His legs, even though I still hear my father ranting and raving. His outbursts were so unpleasant they always felt physical. That's why I went numb. I don't have to do that anymore. This is not my battle but God's."

Are you in an emotional battle? Have you suffered so many blows you feel you have to go through life numb, like a zombie, to keep yourself from feeling pain? If so, a lie lodged itself in your thinking at some point in your life, and you drew a wrong conclusion. Let Jesus replace that conclusion with truth. There is no truth like His. It's irreplaceable. Once instilled in your thinking, it's there forever. Cling to Him. His words will be your protection.

> *"Because he loves me," says the Lord, "I will rescue him; I will protect him, for he acknowledges my name. He will call upon me, and I will answer him; I will be with him in trouble, I will deliver him and honor him* (Ps. 91:14-15)

Life Instead of Death

"I wish I could die!" Delores moaned. She had just finished telling me about herself, how she loved reading and art, and always dreamed she would spend her life as a romantic, happily lost amidst her books and paintings. After a few minutes, however, I realized what she really wanted to talk about was not her dreams but her disappointments. Since leaving her spouse two years before, she hadn't been able to organize her life or her thoughts. Instead of dealing with the present, she was flooded with memories from the past—memories of her mother's threats to put her in a girls' home. Memories of cat fights her mom had with the neighbors. Memories of an uncle who sexually abused her. Memories of a marriage gone sour.

Delores felt sick and in her words "unimportant, unprotected, and smothered by life's experiences." Sobbing, she said, "I want to die!" Reaching for one Kleenex after another, she wiped the tears overflowing her eyes. "Life is horrid."

My heart went out to Delores. Her tears, an outpouring of what was in her heart, made her look vulnerable and lost. As I sat across from her, I knew I didn't have the right words to encourage her, but Jesus did. I suggested she let Him minister to her wounds. Closing her eyes and folding her hands, she leaned back against the chair and prayed. A painter with a visual imagination, Delores was deeply touched when God's response came in pictures.

She spoke quietly and clearly about what she saw in her spirit: "I'm buried alive. Dirt and rocks are all around. I can't move, but I hear something above me. Someone's quickly removing the rocks and dirt. I can see now. It's Jesus. He is brushing debris away from my face. He is breathing life into me, lifting me up. I'm small, about nine months old. His presence is soothing. He's singing lullabies, humming, and whispering to me. His warm arms are around me. They are strong and won't let me go."

As she continued talking, I saw her becoming calm. "Now," she said, "I'm being rocked. The motion is like soothing oil. Jesus will never let go of me. He tells me I don't have to remember those bad memories anymore. They're gone. I can breathe again. My heart's not racing. I don't have to live in darkness or confinement. My spirit will never die. Death holds no boundaries. It doesn't exist; only life exists."

An eagle knows when it's going to die. It flies to a rock, plants its feet there, and looks into the sun. I thought about Delores. Her feet are planted on the Rock, and when God decides it's her time to leave the world, she will look up and see eternal life with the Son of God. Only life exists.

Are your feet planted on the Rock or is the grim reaper lying to you, telling you your disappointments are too many and death is preferable to life? Sin entered the world when Adam and Eve were in the garden. Life *is* horrid at times. However, God sent His son, Jesus, to give us hope and a future. If you let Him whisper the truth into your bruised soul, as Delores did, He will breathe new life into you. You won't ever die.

> *My flesh and my heart may fail, but God is the strength of my heart and my portion forever* (Ps. 73:26).

A Tree Planted by the Water

The phone rang at 11:30 one night. As I groped for the receiver and put it to my ear, I heard my former sister-in-law, Anne, say, "It's serious! I must see you right away!" Encouraging her to come, I climbed out of bed, put on my robe, went downstairs, and sat down to wait for her arrival, wondering what the crisis could possibly be. Shortly the doorbell rang. When I opened the door, there stood Anne, holding a beautiful, blooming flower in her hand. "You woke me up to show me a flower?" I said unappreciatively. "But it's a *Serius* flower," she squealed and burst through the door. "So!" I thought to myself, rather unimpressed and a bit perturbed as I followed her into my kitchen. "It takes seven years to bloom," she said. Now I was awake. "And it only blooms for one night," she added, smiling, with a twinkle in her eye, handing it to me. My unappreciative mouth opened in wonder as it dawned on me that Anne had driven over to my home in the middle of the night because it was me with whom she wanted to share this blessed event. I felt her favor and God's. He used a flower to love me.

He used words to love a woman named Barbara. Like the Serius flower, she was a late bloomer. Neglected as a child, she didn't develop emotionally or socially the way her peers did. Once a week she was so anxious to go to playschool across the street from where she lived that she would run up and down the stairs in her home. Her mother, at just the right time, would fling open the front door. Breathless, Barbara would dash out of her home to the sandbox in which the neighborhood children played. In her memory, though, she saw herself all alone in the sandbox. The other children didn't want to play with her. They would leave, and her heart would sink. She was so lonely.

Barbara needed love, training, and affirmation, but no one was there to give it to her. No one was there to make her feel good about herself or nurture her true identity into existence. Her parents had their own problems and couldn't deal with their child's needs.

When I met Barbara 25 years later, she had become a Christian and was diligently studying the Bible. She came wanting healing from the negative feelings she had about herself. As we prayed, she jumped with both feet into a river of faith. "God, I don't know who I am. In my eyes I'm a zero. I need truth," she said, tremors in her voice. A few seconds passed and in her spirit she heard, "You belong to me. I'm nurturing you. You are like a tree planted by the water with roots that go down deep. The living water, coming from the bottom up, nurtures these roots, and the tree is healthy and growing. It's blooming and blossoming."

Barbara smiled, her thirst for affirmation quenched by the living water.

Do you feel God's affirmation? Are you healthy and growing? Or are you a late bloomer, stuck in the mud with lies? If that's where you are, don't take in the polluted water the world offers. Like Barbara, let your roots be nurtured with the Living Water of truth.

> *Blessed is the man who does not walk in the counsel of the wicked or stand in the way of sinners or sit in the seat of mockers. But his delight is in the law of the Lord, and on his law he meditates day and night. He is like a tree planted by streams of water, which yields its fruit in season and whose leaf does not wither. Whatever he does prospers* (Ps. 1:1-3).

Afterword

The healing of emotional wounds, big and small, has been a God-given gift to me. For most of my life I did not even know that God could heal the distress of my soul. I was used to the discomfort, ignoring the wounding that came my way. For instance, in my childhood I had friends who would say hurtful things to me, such as, "You can't carry a tune" and sarcastic remarks about my smiling all the time. These words were no big deal, or so I thought. Yet for years I was afraid to sing or smile. These digs *were* a big deal! I just didn't know it. The larger, more severe emotional injuries were no easier, of course. Both types of wounds piled up over the decades of my life and blocked the God-given abilities and talents within me.

Hearing God's voice, I was able to make my way through this emotional pile up. I learned to trust Jesus to lead me to the source of my pain. I could feel the sweet balm of His presence and experience His healing in the midst of the awfulness of my memories. Hurt by hurt, trauma by trauma, Jesus healed me by dispelling the lies I had held for so long. In the dark disharmony of my soul, He brought immediate calm to my mind and dispensed truth to my heart. With truth came the ability to forgive. As an artist and writer, the freedom to forgive gave me a fresh burst of creativity, allowing me to produce at a new level what my mind conceived. When I finally understood the truth and expressed forgiveness to those who wounded me, I was able to walk out of my prison of lies with a full pardon.

My ability to create was unlocked, enabling me to write, unimpeded and uninhibited, about childhood memories that gave me great delight and purpose. No longer does pain and fear discolor my childhood. Tasks and confrontations that I used to avoid at all costs, I now face with calmness and determination. Mountains are meant to be climbed, doors are meant to be opened, and gates are meant to be unlocked.

My journey is not over. God continues to lead me into painful places I would sometimes like to avoid. However, I now know that facing these places is NOT a dreadful trek alone down a dark path. Neither is it wallowing in sadness and fear. I have learned that a short, temporary acceptance of the darkness and pain is the fastest way to the light on the other side. David, the supreme psalmist, learned this when he penned these lines: "Yea though I walk through the valley of the shadow of death, I will fear no evil *for thou art with me*; thy rod and thy staff they comfort me" (Ps. 23:4).

Even when the valley is much longer than I would like, more treacherous than I want to bear, and lonelier than I thought possible, the God who reveals Himself stands beside me and I know He is with me. With Him the valleys become gardens of delight and the painful memories seedbeds of new life.

—*Delores Bauer*, artist and author of *Stories From the Irish Wilderness*

ENDNOTES

[i] Ed Smith, *Beyond Tolerable Recovery* (Campbellsville, KY: Family Care Publishing, 2000), 21

[ii] Romans 12:2

[iii] John 8:32

[iv] Steve Fry, *Rekindled Flame* (Multnomah Publishers, Inc., 2002), 117

[v] Psalms 29: 4-9

[vi] A. Moody Stuart, *The Three Marys* (Great Britain: Hazell Watson & Viney Limited, member of the BPCC Group, Aylesbury, Bucks, 1862), 97

[vii] David Wilkerson, *God's Plan to Protect His People in the Coming Depression* (Lindale, TX: Wilkerson Trust Publications, 1998), p. 35

[viii] Ibid, p. 35

[ix] *Weekly Prayer Update from Israel*, July 15, 2002

[x]Bob Sorge, *Dealing With the Rejection and Praise of Man* (Lee's Summit, MO: Oasis House, 1999), 10,11.

[xi] Jim Burns, *Addicted to God* (Ventura, CA: Regal Books from Gospel Light), p. 35.

[xii] Luke 8:48

[xiii] Revelation 22:16

[xiv] Jim Burns, *Handling Your Hormones: The Straight Scoop on Love and Sexuality* (Eugene, OR: Harvest House, 1986), 46, 47

[xv] Lynn Vincent, "Breaking Faith," *World Magazine* (Ashville, NC, 2002), 22

[xvi] Steve Fry, *I Am* (Multnomah Publishers, Inc., 2000), 52

[xvii] John 20: 14-16

[xviii] Henri Nouwen, *The Inner Voice of Love* (New York, New York: Doubleday a division of Random House, Inc., 1996), 45

[xix] Henri J. M. Nouwen, *The Only Necessary Thing* (New York, NY 10017: The Crossroad Publishing Co., 1999), 67

To contact Mary Nelson:
E-mail: mnelsonstl@sbcglobal.net

Printed in the United States
65781LVS00002B/34-57